PUBLISHING

## A Wild Australia Guide

# NATIVE PLANTS

AUTHOR: **CATHY HOPE**
PRINCIPAL PHOTOGRAPHER: **STEVE PARISH**

# Contents

**Left:** Tall Kangaroo Paw (*Anigozanthos flavidus*), Albany Cat's Paw (*A. preissii*) and Everlasting Daisies (*Rhodanthe chlorocephala* var. *rosea*) in Kings Park, Perth. **Right:** Golden Spotted Emu Bush (*Eremophila maculata* var. *aurea*).

# Introduction

Australia's distinctly unique flora creates great interest nationally and internationally. Our rich botanical heritage in all its floral finery is there for all to enjoy and explore. From the coast to the alps and into the vast red centre, a visit to National Parks (NP) and bushland reserves, featuring natural stands of remnant bushland are a sight to behold. Wildflowers are often viewed along country roadsides. Make sure to take time for bush walks as not all wildflowers are bold in their beauty. Search for tiny secretive "gems" such as orchids or view Australian flora at botanical gardens — the choice is endless.

Worldwide, there are approximately 350,000 plant species. Australia has over 24,000 described species. The States with the greatest number of native species are Western Australia with about 7463 and Queensland with around 7535.

This *Wild Australia Guide* aims to give you a "snapshot" selection of iconic wildflowers and trees that provide character to the Australian landscape. Immerse yourself in the images as you browse through the pages of this field guide, and acquire a feel for this land's remarkable flora. Be enticed and stimulated to seek some of the most exceptional flora on this planet.

The largest plant family in Australia is Myrtaceae featuring 70 genera and 1,646 species. There are 3000 species in this family worldwide, which is also known as the Myrtle family. This book includes the genera: *Callistemon*, *Darwinia*, *Eucalyptus*, *Corymbia*, *Kunzea*, *Leptospermum*, *Melaleuca* and *Verticordia* from the Myrtaceae family. Common characteristics of Myrtaceae include prominent stamens and aromatic oil glands.

Another significant and large family in Australia is Proteaceae, with 45 genera and 842 species. There are 1500 species of Proteaceae described throughout the world, with South Africa well known for its Proteaceae genera. This book includes Australian genera: *Banksia*, *Grevillea*, *Hakea*, *Isopogon*, *Macadamia* and *Telopea*. *Macadamia* and *Telopea* genera evolved on the great southern land Gondwana about 100 million years ago, followed by *Banksia*, *Grevillea*, *Hakea* and *Isopogon* genera about 60 million years ago. Every flower in the Proteaceae family has four stamens and generally a long style.

**Top:** Cranbrook Bells. **Opposite, Myrtaceae clockwise from top:** Green Bottlebrush; Graceful Honey-Myrtle; Tick Bush; *Beaufortia aestiva;* Pear-fruited Mallee; Heath Tea-tree. **Opposite, Proteaceae clockwise from top:** Long-styled Grevillea; Tasmanian Waratah; Rose Coneflower; Heath-leaved Banksia; Silky Hakea; Prickly Dryandra.

MYRTACEAE

PROTEACEAE

## FORESTS

Twenty-one per cent of Australia's continent is covered by 163 million hectares of forest — equating to 4% of the world total, with 13% of Australia's forests protected in conservation reserves. Over 50 million years ago, it is believed about half of the world's plants lived in rainforests covering Australia. Reminders of that time exist as remnant ancient Gondwanan forests, today existing as the rainforests of temperate and wet tropical Australia where flowering plants with primitive features remain. It is thought that rainforest covered 8 million hectares of Australia in 1788, now sadly reduced to 2 million hectares. Open wet and dry sclerophyll forests and woodlands are dominated by *Eucalyptus* and *Acacia* species. The ancestors of *Eucalyptus* species evolved in moist rainforests located in the Greater Blue Mountains area, which enjoys 91 *Eucalyptus* species.

## ALPINE

Alpine fields put on glorious wildflower displays during summer. These treasured habitats are found at altitudes above 1800 metres in the States of NSW, Vic and Tas in south-east Australia.

## WATERWAYS

The significance of the Murray Darling River System is the lifeblood of Australia as it drains more than 1 million km$^2$ across four States from its source to the sea.

## COASTAL

Australia, the world's largest island, has a coastline measuring 36,700 km. The coastal fringes accommodate all major cities with 90% of Australia's population located in just 10% of its land mass.

## DESERTS

Australia's arid interior is full of mystery and surprise. For those who haven't been there before, you will discover that much of it, is far from a lifeless desert.

Uluru-Kata Tjuta National Park has 416 native plant species.

Central Australia has been less effected than other areas by invasion of alien flora. A survey revealed that of 719 species sampled, only 25 were introduced plants. The most common being Ruby Dock (*Rumex vesicarius*) which is thought to have come to Australia with cameleers during the 19th century as packing in saddles.

# Vegetation map of Australia

1. OCEANS
   - Mangrove forests
2. FORESTS
   - Tropical rainforest
   - Subtropical rainforest
   - Warm-temperate rainforest
   - Cool-temperate rainforest
   - Cloud forest
   - Wet sclerophyll forest
   - Dry sclerophyll forest
3. TALL AND LOW WOODLANDS
   - Monsoon & tropical woodlands
   - Temperate & other eucalypt woodlands
   - Riverine woodlands
   - Semi-arid shrub with savanna
   - Arid & semi arid low woodlands
4. SHRUBLANDS AND SCRUBLANDS
   - Mallee
   - Acacia – Mulga
   - Acacia – Brigalow
   - Saltbush/Bluebush
5. HEATHS
   - Wallum
   - Temperate
6. GRASSLANDS AND SEDGELANDS
   - Northern grasslands
   - Desert grasslands
   - Temperate grasslands
   - Cool-temperate grasslands
   - Cold-climate grasslands & sedgelands
7. EXTREME HABITATS
   - Alpine herbfields
   - Salt lakes

NOTE: Temperate heath areas are mainly near the coast and too small to show at this scale.

There are many salt lakes in Western Australia — usually long, narrow and meandering. They are too small at this scale to show.

Plant communities are rarely delineated by sharp boundaries. Wildlife also wander across boundaries and find boundary edges to be rich habitats, providing the best shelter as well as diverse food resources. Small-scale maps of this kind should be used as a guide only.

7

# Plant Behaviour

Australia has many attention seeking wildflowers. Some are especially adapted to entice insects — other flowers attract birds.

About 65–80% of flowers are pollinated by insects. Perfumed flowers are for insect attraction — almost 100 Australian orchid species can mimic the pheromone of a female insect, attracting the matching male to assist with pollination. Ants can't resist sickly sweet fragrances of flowers and their visits also assist in the pollination process.

Visual deception is another way for a flower to attract insects — some of Australia's flowers are shaped like butterflies or moths. Insects have ultraviolet vision and flowers exhibit colours in the ultraviolet range beyond our own visible spectrum.

More than half the flowers have honey guides, displaying landing instructions for bees, butterflies and other insects. Twenty five per cent of honey guides are visible to the human eye as spots or stripes, but most can only be seen with ultraviolet vision. Petals on daisies are designed as a landing place for insects. White flowers, lacking colour-attracting pigments, need other methods to attract insects. They can angle their petals directing the sun's warmth to the centre of the flower to bring insect pollinators into this spot.

To most insects, red flowers appear black. This is not the case for birds. Birds have red-sensitive vision. Bright red and yellow flowers have evolved especially for a unique relationship with birds. Also, these flowers are often without perfume and are shaped for nectar probing beaks. *Grevillea* and *Banksia* genera of the Proteaceae family, together with honeyeater birds, evolved about 60 million years ago — they needed each other for survival.

Nature's best plans can go astray. Grevillea flowers have an in-built barrier of hairs to prevent Australia's tiny native bees from robbing the nectar meant for birds. Larger feral bees easily push their way into grevillea flowers, giving birds unexpected competition for the nectar they seek.

**Top:** Scaly-breasted Lorikeet feeding on grevillea.  **Opposite, clockwise from top:** Grass Pyrgimorph Grasshopper on a Yellow Everlasting Daisy; White Spider Orchid displaying honey guides; Eastern Spinebill Honeyeater on grevillea; Royal Bluebell.

# Ecology & Biodiversity

All Australian forests have a thick mat of fungal underlay beneath the soil. Eucalypts would not thrive without a partnership with Ectomycorrhizal fungi — this has been proven in China when eucalypt plantations were in their infancy. Seedlings had to be inoculated with special fungi from Australia to make them flourish.

It is estimated that up to one half of all Australian plants are assisted with propagation by ants. Ants drag seed to their underground nests, eat the fleshy appendages called elaiosomes, then leave the rest of the seed which becomes safely stored in a dark and dry nest, sometimes for years. Germination is activated by heavy soaking rain or in many cases by smoke from a bushfire.

Research has proven that, with some species, more success with germination can be achieved with seeds that have been kept in the dark for several months, e.g. *Epacris* species. Other findings by scientists include the discovery that seed dormancy can be broken and germination activated in over 400 species, by subjecting their seeds to smoke. The chemical "butenolide" in smoke does the trick — it shows how vital bushfire is in the life of Australia's flora.

Ephemerals also have an interesting relationship with their environment. These short-lived annuals, like many everlasting daisies, are "avoiders", with a chemical growth inhibitor preventing germination during times of drought. After heavy soaking rain, carpets of these flowers create a miraculous transformation of the arid land.

As you progress through this guide, you will find many other fascinating relationships Australia's plants have with us and other living creatures.

**Top:** Pom Pom Everlasting (*Cephalipterum drummundii*), Coalseam Conservation Park, Western Australia. **Opposite:** Tick Bush (*Kunzea ambigua*).

# Conservation

Australia has 5031 plant species at risk — that's about 25% of the world's rare, endangered and threatened species. Alarmingly, 45.9% of the 4500 species in D'Entrecasteaux National Park (right) in south-west Australia are in this risk category.

The adverse impact humans, feral animals and alien flora have on the native flora of Australia has been alarming. Loss of habitat for plant species has occurred from clearing the land for farming, road making, mining, forestry, urban and industrial development and from the changing of watercourses. When deep-rooted native vegetation is removed, it causes the water table to rise and increases the salinity of the soil.

The effect global warming is creating now and is estimated to have on flora in the future, is of major concern. It has been observed that some species have altered their flowering patterns. Alpine vegetation is changing and suffering with weed invasion. An alarming prediction — with an increase of 0.5% global warming above the present annual average, 28% of dryandras will become extinct.

Fortunately with education, protective laws and commercial plantings, the practice of raiding wildflowers from the bush for the cut flower trade has been decreasing.

**Above:** Landcare Challenge, Paringa SA — rows of planted seeds to assist with regeneration. **Left:** Drowned Forest — climate changes have had a massive affect on our native vegetation.

Australia's long term planning for conservation includes national projects such as the "Greening Australia 2020 Vision" — which plans to triple commercial tree crops to 3 million hectares, using mainly eucalypts.

## THE FOLLOWING ORGANISATIONS PLAY VITAL CONSERVATION ROLES THROUGHOUT AUSTRALIA:

- Government Quarantine — biosecurity is assisted by very strict quarantine laws monitoring and restricting plant imports.

- Commonwealth Government — established an Environment Protection and Biodiversity Conservation Act and keep a register of rare and threatened plants.

- National and State Botanic Gardens — custodians with living collections of native plants, botanists conducting research, seed banks, cloning threatened species by tissue culture, and flora education.

- CSIRO — created ROTAP (Rare or Threatened Australian Plants) listing 5031 species.

- National Parks and Reserves — protection of remnant vegetation and educating the public.

- Local Councils — monitor vegetation removal, include water saving Australian flora in streetscapes and parklands and encourage the planting of local species.

- Society for Growing Australian Plants — groups all over Australia study, publish information, propagate and reclaim areas with local species.

**Below, left:** Styx Valley, Tasmania, home to the world's tallest hardwood trees is still under threat.
**Below, right:** Degraded landscape — the result of land clearing and chemical pollution and mining of the land, Queenstown, Tasmania.

# Acacia
## Family: Mimosaceae

The *Acacia* genus evolved more than 45 million years ago. The world's 1200–1350 species of *Acacia* grow in Australia, Africa, America and India.

*Acacia*, Australia's largest genus of flowering plants, has 954 species and these iconic plants, illuminating Australia's bushland, are well known as wattles.

Australia is lit up with every shade of yellow imaginable as the flowering of this multitude of species sweeps from place to place. Each pompom or cylinder shaped bloom is made up of 3–130 individual flowers and the fluffy look comes from the stamens on every tiny flower.

*Acacia* species are xerophytes (dry living plants) ranging from low growing shrubs to very tall trees. Many are short lived perennials. All juvenile plants begin with feathery leaves that may ultimately change into water saving phyllodes in a range of diverse leaf-like shapes.

*Acacia* species are legumes with tap roots and nodules accommodating bacteria that fix atmospheric nitrogen, adding nutrients to the soil.

Species of *Acacia* grow wild in every Australian State and most habitats including coast, woodlands, alps, Mulga, mallee, arid zones and even in rainforests. They are pioneer plants, readily naturalising countryside disturbed by man. These hardy plants thrive in a range of conditions including sandy heaths, gravelly soil, water courses and rocky sandstone hillsides.

Wattleseed is a high protein food, traditionally used by Aborigines. It is now gathered for Australia's bushfood industry, grown as a famine food in Africa (Australian species *Acacia colei*) and eaten by parrots and native pigeons.

Squirrel Gliders and Sugar Gliders eat wattle sap, bees eat wattle pollen and honeyeaters drink nectar from tiny phyllode glands. Some wattles are host plants for butterflies and homes for thrips.

Over 70 countries grow plantations of Australia's *Acacia* species for perfume oils, cut flowers, timber, reforestation, to help solve dry-land salinity, and fight soil degradation.

**Top:** The popular Queensland Silver Wattle.

# Golden Wattle *Acacia pycnantha*

*Australia's national colours, green and gold come from the Golden Wattle (Acacia pycnantha), which is also the Commonwealth of Australia's national floral emblem.*

**FEATURES:** Sunny golden flowerheads provide great contrast to the long grass-green phyllodes on the tree. A wildfire can kill a parent plant but stimulates prolific germination.

**HABITAT AND DISTRIBUTION:** Widespread in open eucalypt forests, at times on rocky ground in SA, Vic, ACT and NSW. It is interesting to note that Golden Wattle has naturalised in Tasmania and WA where it is not an indigenous plant.

**ECOLOGY:** Plantations of Golden Wattle are grown overseas for the excellent quality of tannin in the bark and for the cut flower and perfume industries. These Australian trees have escaped in California where they are not regarded as pests but in South Africa they have been declared a weed.

**FLOWERING PERIOD:** Late winter and spring
**HEIGHT:** 3–10 m

**PROPAGATION:** Soak seed in boiling water for an hour — suited to temperate climate, fast growing and frost hardy
**STATUS:** Secure

# Queensland Silver Wattle   *Acacia podalyriifolia*

*Packets of seeds are commercially available for Queensland Silver Wattle (*Acacia podalyriifolia*).*

**FEATURES:** Silvery leaf-like phyllodes give this plant its common name and assist the tree with reduced water loss. Following flowering, flat pods up to 12 cm long are formed.

**HABITAT AND DISTRIBUTION:** Stands of these trees grow near Qld and NSW's beaches and nearby ranges.

**ECOLOGY:** Small nectar seeking birds enjoy taking nectar from glands on the phyllodes and bees seek the pollen from the flowers.

**FLOWERING PERIOD:** Late winter — early summer

**HEIGHT:** 3–8 m

**PROPAGATION:** Seeds germinate in 2–7 weeks — suited to tropical climates in a well drained sunny position, frost hardy in temperate climates

**STATUS:** Secure

# Mimosa Bush   *Acacia farnesiana*

*A global species,* Acacia farnesiana *was named after the Farnese Gardens in Italy where it was first grown in 1611.*

**FEATURES:** The bright yellow pom-pom blooms are about 1 cm wide.

**HABITAT AND DISTRIBUTION:** In Australia Mimosa Bush is mainly above the Tropic of

Capricorn from the west to the east coast in WA, NT and Qld.

**ECOLOGY:** Aborigines find the sharp prickles great for removing splinters. The bark is known for medicinal qualities and the timber is ideal for axe handles and music sticks. Plantations are grown for the perfume industry in France.

**FLOWERING PERIOD:** Winter — spring

**HEIGHT:** Normally 3 m but up to 7 m

**PROPAGATION:** Thrives in dry conditions, good as screen plant

**STATUS:** Secure — rarely abundant

# White Sallow Wattle   *Acacia floribunda*

*White Sallow Wattle (Acacia floribunda) is also known as Gossamer Wattle or White Sally.*

**FEATURES:** Blooms are pale lemon or cream cylindrical flowering spikes, about 5 cm long. Narrow phyllodes and pods are often twice as long as the flower spikes.

**HABITAT AND DISTRIBUTION:** Common beside rivers in tablelands and coastal areas of east Vic, NSW and south Qld.

**ECOLOGY:** Galls sometimes occur on the stems of *Acacia* species. These are caused by night-flying wasps.

**FLOWERING PERIOD:** July — November

**HEIGHT:** Up to 7 m

**PROPAGATION:** Use scarified seed — fast growing suited to coastal environments

**STATUS:** Secure

---

# Silver Wattle   *Acacia lasiocalyx*

*The only place in Australia that Silver Wattle (Acacia lasiocalyx) grows wild is Western Australia.*

**FEATURES:** It is likely that the common name Silver Wattle is due to the silvery white tomentum covering stems. Flowerheads are very attractive sunny yellow cylindrical rods about 3–4 cm long.

**HABITAT AND DISTRIBUTION:** Silver Wattle often forms dense thickets in soils surrounding granite outcrops in south-west botanical areas of Australia.

**ECOLOGY:** This *Acacia* species is well adapted to a climate of extremes with stems protected by a white tomentum coating which is sunscreen protection and insulation for the plant.

**FLOWERING PERIOD:** Late winter — spring

**HEIGHT:** Up to 5 m

**PROPAGATION:** Soak seed for an hour in boiling water before planting

**STATUS:** Secure — some of this tree's habitat has been cleared for wheat growing in WA, safe near granite outcrops

# Actinotus

### Family: Apiaceae

By looking at the world's seventeen *Actinotus* species you could be tricked into thinking they belong to the daisy family. However, in actual fact they belong to the same family as carrots. Australia's sixteen species are well known as flannel flowers. The only other country to have an *Actinotus* species is New Zealand. Actinotus comes from the Greek word "actinos" meaning "like the spokes of a wheel".

The fantastic flannel-like appearance and feel, characteristic of these flowers, comes from the woolly texture of bracts, leaves and stems protecting the plant from heat and moisture loss.

A rare species, *Actinotus paddisonii* growing inland at Bourke, NSW has green flowers and *Actinotus forsynthii* of the upper Blue Mountains, NSW has pinkish mauve flowers.

Several species of flannel flowers are found in heath, open forest and sandstone country on the east coast of NSW and South-East Queensland. Five species occur in south-west Australia from Murchison to Shark Bay growing in heath and granite outcrops. The MacDonnell Ranges in the Northern Territory list Desert Flannel Flower (*Actinotus schwarzii*), a rare and threatened species.

Bush fires promote prolific germination and flowering. Beetles, flies, wasps and possibly other insects are responsible for the pollination of flannel flowers and seed is dispersed by wind.

## Sydney Flannel Flower   *Actinotus helianthi*

*Sydney Flannel Flower is recognised as one of Australia's most important floral icons. This flower became the symbol for NSW's Centenary of Federation on 1 January 2001.*

**FEATURES:** Well-known Sydney Flannel Flower has soft white bracts surrounding a pale green centre composed of many tiny individual flowers.

**HABITAT AND DISTRIBUTION:** Wild populations of Sydney Flannel Flower (*Actinotus helianthi*) are found in poor soils in areas such as, Bega, Katoomba, Narribri, Sydney, Port Macquarie and Coonabarabran in NSW and locations in South-East Queensland.

**ECOLOGY:** We are intrigued by the unique appeal of this Flannel Flower and thus, a thriving cut flower industry has evolved. Tissue culture propagation is carried out by NSW's Mt Annan Botanic Garden for the horticultural trade.

**FLOWERING PERIOD:** Mostly spring

**HEIGHT:** 60–90 cm

**PROPAGATION:** Fresh seed recommended — well drained sandy soil in a sunny position

**STATUS:** Secure — urban development is causing natural stands to decline will grow in abundance after a bushfire

**Opposite, top:** Sydney Flannel Flower. **Clockwise from top left:** Flannel Flower, Girraween National Park, Qld; Flannel flowers on long stems produce seeds that are dispersed by wind; The centre of each flower is composed of many tiny individual flowers; The aptly named White Headed Flannel Flower (*Actinotus leucocephalus*).

# Allocasuarina
## Family: Casuarinaceae

During 1982, a new Australian genus *Allocasuarina*, was created and it included a collection of she-oaks with 61 endemic species. Family and genus names are from the Latin "casuarius" referring to characteristic drooping foliage being like the feathers of a cassowary.

These trees with feathery foliage are actually flowering plants and most species are dioecious with separate female and male plants. Females normally have small red clustered flowers and males have tiny rusty flowers in spikes. After flowering, females produce amazing cone-like, textured and patterned, woody fruit. Trunks have a fire resistant, thickly furrowed cork-like covering for protection.

She-oak species experience many habitats including sand dunes and cliff faces in seaside locations, open forests and woodlands, red sands and rocky outcrops of the arid interior and rainforest margins.

Woody cones from female she-oaks provide seed as a main food source for the Glossy Black Cockatoo, Australia's most endangered cockatoo.

She-oaks are highly valued by Indigenous Australians, for shade, emergency water from the trunk, timber for tools such as, clubs and boomerangs, medicinal remedies and sweet gum for food.

Used for land reclamation in Australia they have also been great ambassadors in countries such as China where over 1 million hectares have been planted.

## Desert Oak   *Allocasuarina decaisneana*

*Desert Oak is a desert tree with great charisma. When in Central Australia, sit quietly near a Desert Oak and listen to the wind whispering through the foliage.*

**FEATURES:** This she-oak has an extremely deep root system to seek water underground. Fantastic textured female cones hold their winged seed securely until cones drop or are burnt.

**HABITAT AND DISTRIBUTION:** These trees grow in red sand and in swales between sand dunes in Central Australia.

**ECOLOGY:** Anangu people living at Uluru say that thin conifer-like juveniles, surrounding a mature tree, represent young males with an elder. For thousands of years they have known how to tap the tree to find trapped water for drinking.

**FLOWERING PERIOD:** Variable

**HEIGHT:** Up to 15 m

**PROPAGATION:** Seed

**STATUS:** Secure — large numbers

# Anigozanthos
## Family: Haemodoraceae

All eleven species, known as kangaroo paws due to their distinctive shape, belong to a small genus *Anigozanthos*, endemic to Western Australia's rich and prolific south-west botanical corner.

The clasping paw-like hands of flowers covered in dense short felt-like hairs, come in a variety of brilliant colours including red, yellow, orange, purple and green.

These tufted perennial herbs protect themselves during extremely hot summers by letting their strap-like leaves die down and underground rhizomes wait until autumn to send leaves up again. Growth of foliage and flowering is even more prolific after a bush fire.

Only Western Australia supports wild populations of kangaroo paws and habitats for these plants in the south-west corner include coastal sandplains, heath and woodlands.

Pollination of kangaroo paws is assisted by minute Honey Possums, wattlebirds and honeyeaters. As they move from flower to flower probing the long flower tubes for nectar, they are brushed with pollen.

Western Australian Aborigines dug up kangaroo paw rhizomes as a source of food. Many stunningly attractive varieties of kangaroo paw are now on the market. These can be used as feature plants when landscaping gardens and commercial crops of kangaroo paw are grown mainly for export to Japan for the cut flower trade.

## Red and Green Kangaroo Paw
*Anigozanthos manglesii*

*Red and Green Kangaroo Paw has special status as Western Australia's floral emblem and for many years has proudly promoted WA's floral heritage.*

**FEATURES:** The bright red stems invite honeyeaters and wattlebirds to land on them and probe the brilliant green furry floral tubes for nectar.

**HABITAT AND DISTRIBUTION:** These striking plants make a stunning display in sandy coastal areas bordering the Southern and Indian Oceans from Manjimup in the south and almost up to Shark Bay. They are also found in bushland surrounding Perth.

**ECOLOGY:** Underground rhizomes were a food source for Aborigines.

**FLOWERING PERIOD:** Winter — spring

**HEIGHT:** 50 cm–1 m

**PROPAGATION:** Seed, or divide rhizomes in autumn

**STATUS:** Secure — common and Protected

**Opposite, top:** Cat's Paw. **Clockwise from top:** Red and Green Kangaroo Paw are great ambassadors for Australia; Red and Green Kangaroo Paw; Horticulturists are developing many colour variations with hybrids of *A. manglesii* as shown in the last two images.

# Banksia
## Family: Proteaceae

Australia is home to 76 species of *Banksia*. The genus *Banksia* is named after Sir Joseph Banks who collected Saw Leaf Banksia (*Banksia serrata*) specimens from Australia's east coast during 1770 when accompanying Captain James Cook on the *Endeavour*. The only known complete collection of the world's 76 *Banksia* species is growing at Mt Barker Banksia Farm at Porongurup, in Western Australia's South-West.

Banksia flowering spikes are stunning, often with thousands of individual flowers patterned symmetrically into conical, globular and cylindrical shapes. Blooms come in shades of orange, tan, lemon, yellow, green, red, brown, silver and purple. Banksia shrubs and trees have incredible leaf shape diversity and tough cones which normally require heat from a fire for seed release. Masses of fine proteoid roots search for moisture and nutrients, giving plants a better chance of survival in impoverished soils.

Banksias are found all over Australia, except in Central Australia, mainly in sandy coastal situations, heath, mallee, open forest and mountain ranges. Swamp Banksia (*Banksia dentata*), the only banksia native to the Top End of Australia, grows in low-lying flats flooded during the wet season.

Pollination of banksias is assisted by nectar feeding bats, Honey Possums, Eastern Pygmy-possums, ring-tailed possums, and birds such as honeyeaters, lorikeets, cockatoos and wattlebirds. Aborigines used dry cones as hair brushes. They also soaked banksia blooms to make a sweet drink from the nectar and European pioneers and settlers boiled blooms to make cough syrup.

## Coast Banksia    *Banksia integrifolia*

*Coast Banksia is often planted as a street tree in coastal regions. It has evolved to cope with salt spray and fierce winds. Coast Banksia is the floral emblem for the city of Frankston, Victoria.*

**FEATURES:** Cylindrical flowerheads are creamy lemon followed at maturity with cones that look quite comical when many of their follicles have opened to release the seed.

**HABITAT AND DISTRIBUTION:** Frequently found growing right beside the shore, these trees provide great shelter in windy environments. It grows wild at places such as Fraser Island, Qld, and is seen around the coastline of Qld, NSW, Vic and Tas.

**ECOLOGY:** Ring-tailed possums, Eastern Pygmy-possums and gliders enjoy the nectar provided by flowers of Coastal Banksia.

**FLOWERING PERIOD:** Late summer — winter

**HEIGHT:** Normally to 12 m but sometimes up to 25 m

**PROPAGATION:** Seed — frost hardy

**STATUS:** Secure

**Opposite, top:** Saw Leaf Banksia. **Clockwise from top:** Coast Banksia can tolerate salt spray; Saw Leaf Banksia; Coast Banksia seed pod.

# Scarlet Banksia

*Banksia coccinea*

Scarlet Banksia has another common name, "Red Combs". This sensational superbly patterned banksia grows exclusively in Western Australia's remarkable South-West botanical area.

**FEATURES:** Red styles emerge from silky silvery buds giving the bloom a spectacular appearance.

**HABITAT AND DISTRIBUTION:** Grows wild on deep sandy plains with a limestone base in WA's Barren, Albany and Stirling botanical districts.

**ECOLOGY:** Populations of Scarlet Banksia have declined due to the disease *Phytophthora cinnamomi*.

**FLOWERING PERIOD:** Most of year but mainly winter — summer

**HEIGHT:** 1.5–4 m

**PROPAGATION:** Seed — difficult to grow in eastern States

**STATUS:** Secure — over picked for the cut flower trade in the past, commercial picking is now banned on crown land

# Wallum Banksia

*Banksia aemula*

Wallum Banksia was one of the first Banksia *species to be introduced to England where it could be bought from nurseries by the late 1780s. It has remained a popular plant in cultivation and now has raised status as the floral emblem of Queensland's Gold Coast City.*

**FEATURES:** Flowers are greenish-yellow and leaves have toothed margins.

**HABITAT AND DISTRIBUTION:** Enjoys a coastal environment often growing wild on sand dunes in Qld and NSW.

**ECOLOGY:** Honeyeaters seek nectar from the flowers of Wallum Banksia.

**FLOWERING PERIOD:** Autumn — winter

**HEIGHT:** Averages 3 m but can grow up to 8 m

**PROPAGATION:** Seed and cuttings

**STATUS:** Secure — though threats include coastal land development and the disease *Phytophthora cinnamomi*

# Cut-leaf Banksia *Banksia praemorsa*

*If Cut-leaf Banksia is destroyed by fire, it can and will regenerate from seed.*

**FEATURES:** Sensational bright red cylindrical spikes more than compensate for this plant that has an unpleasant aroma, said to smell like rotten meat pies.

**HABITAT AND DISTRIBUTION:** Grows naturally near the shore and on seaside cliffs between Albany and Cape Riche in Western Australia.

**ECOLOGY:** It would be interesting to know why Nature gave this plant an offensive smell. Perhaps it is to ward off predators or it may even be to attract a certain Insect.

**FLOWERING PERIOD:** Winter — early summer

**HEIGHT:** Up to 4 m

**PROPAGATION:** Seed and cuttings

**STATUS:** Vulnerable, restricted habitat — threatened by disease *Phytophthora cinnamomi*

# Acorn Banksia *Banksia prionotes*

*Acorn Banksia occurs in South-West Western Australia.*

**FEATURES:** Silvery-white flower buds begin opening from the base of the bloom exposing orange styles creating an acorn-like appearance.

**HABITAT AND DISTRIBUTION:** Found from Shark Bay down to Perth growing in deep sandy locations.

**ECOLOGY:** Each bloom regulates the opening of tiny flowers providing nectar seekers with a more sustained supply and assisting in the pollination process.

**FLOWERING PERIOD:** Late summer — autumn — winter

**HEIGHT:** Up to 10 m

**PROPAGATION:** Seed — plants appreciate a limestone base

**STATUS:** Secure — widespread; threatened by disease *Phytophthora cinnamomi*

# Blandfordia

Family: Blandfordiaceae

*Blandfordia*, the only genus in the family Blandfordiaceae, was named in 1804 after the Marquis of Blandford (George Spencer Churchill). He supported botany and had a magnificent garden at Blenheim Palace in England. The common name adopted for all four species of these festive flowers is Christmas Bell.

Flame coloured *Blandfordia* species with up to twenty waxy tubular bells per stem, flower right through summer. Plants are perennial herbs with strap-like leaves and underground rhizomes.

Australia's east coast is the only place where Blandfordia species grow wild in damp sand and peat, acidic soils in heathland and swampy areas.

Northern Christmas Bell (*Blandfordia grandiflora*) occurs at latitudes between 24–34 degrees south in Qld and NSW and Christmas Bell (*Blandfordia nobilis*) is found at latitudes between 34–36 degrees south in NSW. The now very rare Mountain Christmas Bell (*Blandfordia cunninghamii*) grows in moist sandstone crevices in NSW's Blue Mountains and at Mount Kembla, Illawarra.

Three species on the east-coast of mainland Australia have been severely depleted due to over picking from the wild for the sale of Christmas flowers. Even more threatening, much of their coastal habitat has been cleared and developed for towns and cities. Australia's export of cultivated Christmas Bells to Japan began in 1991. Now countries such as Zimbabwe and Israel also cultivate and market these attractive flowers.

## Tasmanian Christmas Bell  *Blandfordia punicea*

*Tasmania's endemic Christmas Bell has been depicted on a 50 cent Australian postage stamp. The festive flowering of thousands of wild plants brightens the landscape at Zeehan and other places for Christmas.*

**FEATURES:** Bell shaped flowers are red on the outside and yellow inside.

**HABITAT AND DISTRIBUTION:** Widely distributed in western Tasmania's high rainfall areas on damp moors and heaths from the coast to the subalpine central highlands.

**ECOLOGY:** Pollination of this species is carried out by birds, mainly honeyeaters.

**FLOWERING PERIOD:** October — March

**HEIGHT:** Up to 1 m

**PROPAGATION:** Seed or by division of rhizomes in spring — grow in 50% peat and 50% washed sand, most difficult *Blandfordia* species to cultivate

**STATUS:** Secure — Protected — not threatened to the same extent as the mainland species

**Opposite, top:** Tasmanian Christmas Bell.  **Above:** The Tasmanian Christmas Bell flower spike is erect, to 1 m high. It has a head of red bells with yellow tips.

# Boronia
## Family: Rutaceae

Oranges, lemons and *Boronia* species all belong to the fragrant citrus family Rutaceae. Named after 18th Century plant collector, Francesco Borone, *Boronia* is Australia's largest representative genus of this interesting family. Australia has about 100 species and New Caledonia has four species.

The Hunter Region Botanic Garden in New South Wales has established a "Boronia Garden".

Cup or bell-shaped flowers have four petals and eight stamens and only a few species have really fragrant flowers. Flowers come in white, yellow, brown/yellow, blue and many shades of pink and mauve. Most species have leaves with aromatic oil glands. Some have a dreadful smell, thought to be nature's way of stopping animals from grazing on the foliage. Tasmania's endemic Lemon-scented Boronia (*Boronia citriodora*) smells like lemons when the leaves are crushed.

Over half of Australia's boronias occur in Western Australia, especially in the South-West corner. Eastern and northern species from the coast to higher altitudes are found among other flowering shrubs in the undergrowth of dry sclerophyll forests, in heath, open woodland, and moist habitats growing beside rivers and in gullies.

*Boronia* species plants have adapted to and have the ability to regenerate soon after bushfires.

## Brown Boronia    *Boronia megastigma*

*Brown Boronia is world famous due to its sensational fragrant flowers which are commercially grown for the floristry trade, garden plants and for extraction of oil for perfume.*

**FEATURES:** Small rounded bell shaped flowers are arranged along each fine stem. Chocolate brown on the outside petals contrast with the gold on the inside.

**HABITAT AND DISTRIBUTION:** Wild plants grow in Western Australia's Albany botanical area in swampy sands.

**ECOLOGY:** Australia grows commercial crops of Brown Boronia (*Boronia megastigma*), but the demand is so high overseas that other countries also grow large quantities including Europe, Israel, South Africa, New Zealand and the State of California, USA.

**FLOWERING PERIOD:** Winter — spring

**HEIGHT:** Up to 2 m

**PROPAGATION:** Seed or cuttings in summer

**STATUS:** Secure — less common due to wild harvesting

**Opposite, top:** Pink Boronia (*Boronia thujona*).
**Above:** The world famous Brown Boronia.

# Brunonia
## Family: Goodeniaceae

It's always a welcome surprise to come across these wonderful "true blue" Australian flowers — Blue Pincushion (*Brunonia australis*) — whether they are seen as isolated plants or massed in a huge patch of blue. The *Brunonia* genus has a single species Blue Pincushion sometimes called Native Cornflower. This genus is named after the famous British botanist Robert Brown (1773-1858) who explored Australia's rich botany, leaving the world a great legacy of plant knowledge. The *Brunonia* genus has been changed from the plant family Brunoniaceae to Goodeniaceae.

Hemispherical sky-blue flowerheads up to 2 cm wide are composed of tiny tubular flowers each with five deep blue petals. The golden "pins" protruding from the cushion are anthers surrounding each style.

Rosettes of slightly hairy grey-green leaves surround the bases of stems of these perennial herbs.

Blue Pincushion is widely distributed throughout most parts of Australia. It's found on red sand dunes, gravelly soils, grassy woodlands and dry sclerophyll forests. It has avoided tropical Australian habitats.

Patches of wild *Brunonia australis* are at risk when native bushland is cleared for farming and housing estates. These flowers used to be abundant in the north-east of Tasmania and now have a more restricted distribution.

## Blue Pincushion    *Brunonia australis*

**FLOWERING PERIOD:** Winter — summer

**HEIGHT:** Up to 50 cm

**PROPAGATION:** Seed in well drained soil, sunny position; division July — August

**STATUS:** Do not have Threatened status on the mainland

**Opposite:** Blue Pincushion (*Brunonia australis*) is a "true blue" Australian flower. **Above:** Patches of *B. australis* are at risk where bushland is cleared.

# Calandrinia
## Family: Portulacaceae

Chile and North America share with Australia more than 150 species belonging to the *Calandrinia* genus. This genus is named after Jean Louis Calandrini, a Swiss botanist of the 18th century. Australia's 60 plus species, some without names as yet, are known collectively as "parakeelya". The word parakeelya is derived from Aboriginal dialects — Eastern Arrernte people use "*parrkelye*", Pitjantjatjara people refer to "*parkilypa*" and Walpiri people say "*parrkillyi*".

During 1998, botanist Hershkovitz proposed a new genus *Parakeelya*, but there is still research and debate as to whether the genus *Calandrinia* should be changed.

Parakeelyas have evolved as ephemerals — drought avoiders. Seeds stubbornly remain dormant, only awakening when there is enough moisture to sustain a life cycle. Regeneration after a bushfire is generally very prolific.

These little charmers sprinkle their flowers in carpets over the red sands in spinifex country of arid and semi-arid Australia. Central Australia has at least eleven species.

For thousands of years Indigenous people have harvested the raw leaves for their water content as well as a food source. Leaves are also boiled as a vegetable and cooked seeds are ground for cake making. Some pioneers and early settlers to Australia also boiled the green leaves for their meals.

Blue-tongue Skinks, feral camels and cattle are known to graze on parakeelya foliage.

## Broad-leafed Parakeelya    *Calandrinia balonensis*

*Broad-leafed Parakeelya brightens up Australia's red sandy areas soon after soaking rain.*

**FEATURES:** Eye-catching magenta coloured soft flowers appear on these low growing succulents soon after germination. Purple pigment in the petals of flowers is a method of sunscreen protection.

**HABITAT AND DISTRIBUTION:** This succulent is widely distributed in dry inland Australia growing in red sand.

**ECOLOGY:** When analysed, fleshy leaves of *Calandrinia balonensis* have been found to be 93% water and are said to be 100% edible.

**FLOWERING PERIOD:** Any time of the year especially after heavy winter rain

**HEIGHT:** Up to 25 cm

**PROPAGATION:** Seed — require well drained sand in full sun

**STATUS:** Secure

**Opposite, top:** Broad-leafed Parakeelyas carpet the red sands of dry inland Australia. **Clockwise from top:** Yellow Saltspoon Daisies (*Leucochrysum stipitatum*) grow among Broad-leafed Parakeelyas; Round-leaved Parakeelya; Parakeelyas grow when there is enough water for sustenance.

# Callistemon

### Family: Myrtaceae

Australia has 34 of the world's 38 *Callistemon* species with the other four in New Caledonia. This remarkable bottlebrush group, was named by botanist Robert Brown while on voyage to "Terra Australis" with Matthew Flinders during 1814. Callistemon comes from Greek words "callos" meaning beautiful and "stemon" meaning stamen. Mt Annan Botanic Garden in New South Wales has a feature garden displaying more than 30 species, plus many cultivars of callistemons. There are moves to transfer *Callistemon* species into the *Melaleuca* genus.

A callistemon bloom is composed of many individual flowers with masses of sensational stamens looking like the bristles of a bottlebrush. Callistemon stamens are separate from each other compared to the flower of a melaleuca, which has stamens in bundles of five. Plants have narrow pointed leaves and vary from shrubs to tall trees up to 10 metres in height.

Nearly all species are concentrated in high rainfall coastal temperate regions of east and south-east Australia with only two species in Western Australia's South-West. Naturally damp locations like swamps and riverbanks are preferred habitats. In the Northern Territory in mountain ranges of Central Australia, Desert Bottlebrush (*Callistemon pauciflous*) grow in rocky gorges.

Bird attracting callistemons, a great favourite with gardeners throughout Australia, are also cultivated in other parts of the world including Kathmandu Valley in the Himalayan Mountains of Nepal.

## Red Bottlebrush   *Callistemon citrinus*

*Red Bottlebrush, is considered to be the most widely cultivated callistemon.*

**FEATURES:** The fragrance from oil glands in the lemon-scented leaves give this small tree the species name *citrinus*. Scientists are researching oil extracts from callistemons to discover suitable natural herbicides.

**HABITAT AND DISTRIBUTION:** These wild coastal plants have a widespread distribution in swampy areas of NSW, extending across State borders to Victoria's Gippsland and into Queensland.

**ECOLOGY:** Some of the early settlers to Australia used the leaves steeped in boiling water to make a lemon flavoured tea.

**FLOWERING PERIOD:** November — December and March — April

**HEIGHT:** Up to 6 m

**PROPAGATION:** Seed and cuttings

**STATUS:** Secure — common and widespread

**Opposite, top:** Gold-tipped Bottlebrush (*Callistemon polandii*).
**Clockwise from top:** Red Bottlebrush should be lightly pruned
and fertilised after flowering.

# Lemon Bottlebrush   *Callistemon pallidus*

*Lemon Bottlebrush, a frost tolerant plant, has been cultivated in southern England for many years.*

**FEATURES:** Bottlebrush blooms are lemony-cream. December is the flowering time for Lemon Bottlebrush in Tasmania and islands north-east of Tasmania.

**HABITAT AND DISTRIBUTION:** Damp stream-side locations and rocky sites in east coast ranges of temperate Australia support Lemon Bottlebrush. It snows in some of the places where it grows.

**ECOLOGY:** Small marsupials, such as gliding possums, frequent flowering callistemons at night to feed on the nectar.

**FLOWERING PERIOD:** Late spring — summer — autumn

**HEIGHT:** Usually to 3 m, some up to 6 m

**PROPAGATION:** Seed and cuttings — plant in a sunny position, hardy

**STATUS:** Secure — widespread

# Albany Bottlebrush   *Callistemon glaucus*

*Albany Bottlebrush is one of the only two endemic callistemons in Western Australia.*

**FEATURES:** These shrubs have closely packed crimson bottlebrush–like blooms.

**HABITAT AND DISTRIBUTION:** This moisture loving plant is found in Western Australia's South-West in the Albany botanical region growing on the wet edges of swamps and sometimes right in the water.

**ECOLOGY:** Seeds normally remain encased in woody globular nuts along the stem, sometimes for years — an adaption to prevent overcrowding of the species. Heat from a bushfire causes them to be released.

**FLOWERING PERIOD:** Spring — summer

**HEIGHT:** Up to 2 m

**PROPAGATION:** Seed — plant in full sun, appreciates regular watering but copes in drier situations

**STATUS:** Secure — common

# Willow Bottlebrush   *Callistemon salignus*

*Wherever Willow Bottlebrush grows naturally it plays a vital role in helping with the health of the area.*

**FEATURES:** This tall callistemon with creamy–white bottlebrush spikes has a weeping habit and the trunk is covered by white papery bark.

**HABITAT AND DISTRIBUTION:** Enjoying the same conditions as willows, these trees thrive beside freshwater streams and lakes. They have a limited range in Queensland from Maroochydore to near Moreton Bay.

**ECOLOGY:** With water filtering ability, Willow Bottlebrush has been planted in wetlands on the north coast of NSW to improve water quality.

**FLOWERING PERIOD:** Spring — summer
**HEIGHT:** 5–10 m
**PROPAGATION:** Seed
**STATUS:** Secure — widespread

# Wallum Bottlebrush   *Callistemon pachyphyllus*

*Wallum Bottlebrush is an endemic plant confined to eastern Australia.*

**FEATURES:** This small compact shrub has striking red blooms and there is a variant with green blooms.

**HABITATS AND DISTRIBUTION:** Queensland and New South Wales have areas of coastal vegetation called Wallum and *Callistemon pachyphyllus* grows wild here mainly in dampish places.

**ECOLOGY:** When flowering, Wallum Bottlebrush attracts the attention of many nectar feeding birds such as wattlebirds and honeyeaters.

**FLOWERING PERIOD:** Spring — summer — autumn
**HEIGHT:** Up to 1.5 m
**PROPAGATION:** Seed and cuttings — hardy, needs full sun
**STATUS:** Secure

# Correa
## Family: Rutaceae

Australia has eleven species belonging to the endemic genus *Correa*, named after 19th century Portuguese botanist, José Francisco Correa de Serra. Correas, sometimes called Australian Fuchsias, bring welcome winter delight to bush walkers and nectar seeking birds. Correas are in the same family as *Boronia* and *Citrus* species of plants.

Flowers, with four petals mostly fused into a narrow tubular bell, come in shades of white, pink, red, salmon, orange, yellow, green or colour combinations. White Correa (*Correa alba*) differs from other species as it has a shallow bell with spreading petals. Some of these evergreen woody shrubs have rough sandpaper-like leaves and when crushed, most release aromas from oil glands, some smelling like turpentine.

*Correa* species are mainly found in temperate south-east Australia in coastal heathlands and ranges also in rocky woodland soils. The genus is well represented on Kangaroo Island, SA, with at least four species.

Aromatic leaves of White Correa (*Correa alba*) were used hundreds of years ago by seafaring sealers in Bass Strait as a tea substitute.

Most of the eleven *Correa* species have interesting variants with hybrids occurring naturally between species. The Australian National Botanic Gardens has a collection of 60 species and variants. About 120 varieties and cultivars are grown by Denbly Gardens at Killarney in Victoria.

## Native Fuchsia  *Correa reflexa*

*Native Fuchsia is Australia's most well-known* Correa *species with at least twenty wild variants.*

**FEATURES:** Plants range from prostrate ground cover to tallish shrubs with bell shaped flowers to about 4 cm long in reds and greens.

**HABITAT AND DISTRIBUTION:** Tas, Vic, SA, NSW and Qld have wild populations found on coastal dunes, sandy heath, stony hillsides, dry sclerophyll forest and semi-arid areas.

**ECOLOGY:** *Correa reflexa* creates much interest for gardeners as it is winter flowering, frost, drought and sea spray resistant and attracts nectar-feeding birds.

**FLOWERING PERIOD:** Autumn, winter and profuse flowering in spring

**HEIGHT:** Mostly from 0.3–1.5 m, some known to reach 3 m

**PROPAGATION:** Cuttings

**STATUS:** Secure — widespread

**Opposite, top:** The distinctive bell of an Australian Fuchsia (*Correa* sp.).  **Above:** Native Fuchsia is free from pests and diseases and offers a good show of flowers.

# Cycas
## Family: Cycadaceae

Australia is home to 26 of the world's 99 species of *Cycas*, the only genus in the family Cycadaceae. These ancient plants, a legacy from Triassic and Jurassic times, are frequently called cycads. Vietnam, the Philippines, Japan, India and East Africa are some other countries with cycads. Cycas comes from the Greek word "koikas" meaning "a kind of palm". *Cycas* species look like palms but are not related. A display of cycads can be seen at the Brisbane and Adelaide Botanic Gardens.

Cycads belonging to the plant group Gymnospermae, are non-flowering plants with fern-like fronds and seed bearing cones. Female and male plants are dioecious, each gender having separate plants.

*Cycas* species are found in open forest, sandy loams and granite outcrops of tropical Australia. Daintree Rainforest has 21% of Australia's *Cycas* species.

Foliage of *Cycas* species contains the poison cycasin, a serious form of plant defence, that can cause nerve damage to foragers. For thousands of years cycad seeds have been wild harvested as an important food source for Indigenous Australians. Aboriginal women leech out the dangerous toxin then roast and grind the seeds. The future of cycads depend on the continued existence of specific weevils and beetles, the pollinators of these plants, which most likely evolved at the same time many millions of years ago.

## Fire Fern    *Cycas armstrongii*

*Fire Fern is a prolific plant of Litchfield National Park, NT.*

**FEATURES:** A female Fire Fern forms golf ball-like sporophylls, which are fruit hanging from the crown. Spiral scales on the male cone of a Fire Fern open to eject fine spores. This species of *Cycas* has a stout trunk with snake skin-like markings.

**HABITAT AND DISTRIBUTION:** Fire Fern is found in the NT south-west of Darwin from the Finniss River to the Arnhem Highway and the Kimberley region in far north WA.

**ECOLOGY:** Fire Fern, like many other *Cycas* species readily survives the traditional burning off practice during the dry season by growing fresh incandescent green fronds.

**FLOWERING PERIOD:** N/A

**HEIGHT:** Up to 4 m — plants to 6 m are rare

**PROPAGATION:** Seed

**STATUS:** Secure — common, estimated population of 10 million

**Opposite, top:** A cycad (*Cycas calcicola*), Tolmer Falls, NT.
**Clockwise from top:** Young Fire Fern; Common Brushtail Possum;
Sporophylls of female Fire Fern; Male cone of Fire Fern.

# Dampiera
## Family: Goodeniaceae

Western Australia has almost two thirds of 66 named species belonging to *Dampiera*, a genus endemic to Australia.

Captain William Dampier sailed HMS *Roebuck* to Western Australia in 1699 and collected many wildflower specimens including *Dampiera*, a genus that ultimately bore his name. The blue flowers of New Holland, now called Australia, surprised him.

Australia celebrates some of the most beautiful botanical blues, the dominant flower colour, in the *Dampiera* genus. Only a few species are white, pink and yellow. Five heart shaped petals make up each flower.

These frost tolerant plants vary between perennial herbs, often trailing and prostrate or small erect shrubs, with foliage sometimes covered with tomentum.

Many plants self propagate spreading by suckering.

Wild populations of dampiera are mainly concentrated in Western Australia's South-West corner, thriving in deep sandy soils of coastal heath, in woodland, open forest and on the margins of swamps. Tasmania's only species is *Dampiera stricta*, a coastal plant also found in Vic, NSW and Qld. Central Australia and NT have three desert growing species.

The *Dampiera* genus is closely related to *Lechenaultia*, *Goodenia* and *Scaevola*. A surprising feature of all these flowers is that they are able to collect pollen in a two lipped style-cup circling the stigma, prior to the flower opening.

Dampiera plants are widely propagated for the plant nursery trade, much loved for their sensational blues and spreading nature.

## Common Dampiera — *Dampiera linearis*

*Common Dampiera is sold in plant nurseries with the name "Violet Princess".*

**FEATURES:** Plants spread out rapidly reaching about one metre diameter. Violet-blue flowers are prolific.

**HABITAT AND DISTRIBUTION:** Spreading patches of Common Dampiera (*Dampiera linearis*) feature in bushland from Geraldton down to the South-West coast of Western Australia.

**ECOLOGY:** William Dampier was the first person to remark on the many intense blue wildflowers of Western Australia's flora. Deep blue and purple flowers have evolved with in-built sun-screening pigments, for places as sunny as WA.

**FLOWERING PERIOD:** Winter — spring

**HEIGHT:** Up to 50 cm

**PROPAGATION:** Cuttings or division of suckers — plant in sandy soil in full sun

**STATUS:** Secure

**Opposite, top:** *Dampiera stricta.* **Top:** Common Dampieras
(*D. linearis*) nestle among a profusion of other species.
**Above:** Common Dampiera is found in plant nurseries everywhere.

# Darwinia
## Family: Myrtaceae

Over 60 species of *Darwinia*, known as Mountain Bells, are endemic to Australia with nearly 50 in Western Australia.

This genus is named after Charles Darwin's grandfather, Dr Erasmus Darwin (1731–1802).

The flowerheads are very diverse in structure. Rose Darwinia (*Darwinia purpurea*) has a beautiful rosy-red compound centre surrounded by small bracts. Pom-pom Darwinia (*Darwinia vestita*), growing between Albany and Esperance, has white pom-pom compound flowerheads. Many species have bell-shaped blooms with large colourful bracts. Most of these shrubs, from 20–300 cm high, are evergreen, some with aromatic foliage. The leaves of some species redden towards autumn.

Some of the main places where Mountain Bells grow in Western Australia include the Murchison River sandplains and the Porongurup, Barren and Stirling Ranges where they grow on rocky slopes and peaks. A few species are endemic to eastern Australia in SA, Vic and NSW. They are found on the southern and central tablelands and central coast of NSW.

Alarm bells are ringing for almost 50% of *Darwinia* species threatened with extinction. The killing disease Cinnamon Fungus (*Phytophthora cinnamomi*), unexpected fires, prolonged drought and diminishing natural habitats due to land clearing and grazing are all contributing to the endangered or vulnerable status of these plants. WA's Stirling Range's Cranbrook Bell (*Darwinia meeboldii*) is classified as vulnerable, facing a high risk of extinction in the wild in the medium-term future.

## Yellow Mountain Bell    *Darwinia collina*

*The only place that Yellow Mountain Bell can be seen in the wild is the Stirling Range National Park.*

**FEATURES:** Small shrub with crowded leaves and yellow bell-shaped flowers.

**HABITAT AND DISTRIBUTION:** Endemic to the Stirling Range National Park in Western Australia, Yellow Mountain Bell grows in mallee heath and thicket on well drained slopes of Bluff Knoll.

**ECOLOGY:** There are very few Yellow Mountain Bells growing in the wild and there is a risk of them disappearing over the next 20–50 years.

**FLOWERING PERIOD:** Late winter — spring

**HEIGHT:** Up to 1 m

**PROPAGATION:** Cutting prove more successful if grafted onto hardy *Darwinia citriodora*

**STATUS:** Endangered — high risk of extinction in the near future

**Opposite, top:** Cranbrook Bell is facing the risk of extinction in the wild. **Above:** Yellow Mountain Bell can only be found in WA.

# Dendrobium

## Family: Orchidaceae

The world's largest family of flowering plants is Orchidaceae with over 30,000 species. The *Dendrobium* genus has more than 1000 species worldwide. Australia has over 70 species and New Zealand possesses a single endemic species, *Dendrobium cunninghamii*.

Attractive flowers, often hanging in sprays, can be waxy and come in white, cream, yellow, pink, red, mauve and purple. The orchid's lower lip, a labellum, has three lobes most often marked with contrasting colourful blotches, spots or stripes. Some *Dendrobium* species have a lovely fragrance especially *Dendrobium adae* from North Queensland. These evergreen orchids have leaves protruding from the apex of long fleshy storage rhizomes called pseudobulbs.

The *Dendrobium* genus has the greatest number of epiphytic orchids in Australia growing on the branches and trunks of tall trees, tree ferns and paper barks. Roots of epiphytes absorb food and moisture from the air. Some *Dendrobium* species are lithophytic, establishing large clumps on boulders and cliff faces. These eastern orchids thrive in places with high summer rainfall at the coast, on tablelands, in open forests and cool temperate and tropical rainforests. They are found in Tasmania, Victoria, New South Wales, Queensland and the Torres Strait Islands.

The interest in native orchids is enormous in Australia with over 150 Orchid Societies, and as dendrobiums are easy to grow, all 70 species of dendrobiums are under cultivation, often grown in humid glasshouses. Australian National Botanic Gardens has a large collection of Australian orchids from many genera.

## Cooktown Orchid  *Dendrobium phalaenopsis*

*On 19 November 1959, the Cooktown Orchid was declared Queensland's floral emblem during centenary celebrations.*

**FEATURES:** Moth shaped flowers are mainly mauve-pink but can also be lavender or nearly white. Each stem has up to twenty flowers.

**HABITAT AND DISTRIBUTION:** This epiphytic orchid grows wild on trees such as paperbarks in vine thickets or savanah woodland from the Johnston River to Iron Range on the east coast of Cape York. It also grows on the Torres Strait Islands.

**ECOLOGY:** People have caused the decline of Cooktown Orchid in some areas by raiding plants from the wild.

**FLOWERING PERIOD:** Dry season from March — July

**HEIGHT:** Up to 80 cm

**PROPAGATION:** Slab or pot, requires daily water spray and winter warmth

**STATUS:** Endangered — now Rare near Cooktown, Protected

**Opposite, top:** Golden Arch Orchid (*Dendrobium chrysotoxum*).
**Above:** The Cooktown Orchid, Queensland's floral emblem, is magnificent.

# Dryandra
## Family: Proteaceae

Dryandra specimens were first collected during 1791 when the sailing ship HMS *Discovery* landed at King George Sound near Albany in Western Australia. Botanist Robert Brown named this genus in 1810, after Swedish Jonas Dryander, who worked as a botanist librarian for Sir Joseph Banks. Australia has 93 endemic species of *Dryandra* and most can be seen growing at Mount Barker Banksia Farm, near Porongurup in Western Australia.

In late 2007, botanists Mast and Thiele placed *Dryandra* species into the *Banksia* genus due to recent discoveries that these visually different flowers actually evolved from banksias millions of years ago.

Blooms have some similarities to South Africa's proteas or Australia's banksias. Many have dense terminal heads and others are framed by radiating leaves. Colours include orange, yellow, cream, pink, greenish and silvery shades. Plants vary from small prostrate to spreading erect shrubs, some to six metres tall.

Soils with a limestone base are favoured by dryandras where they grow in sandy heath, jarrah forests and woodlands, restricted to south-west Australia.

We know that these ancient plants had a wider distribution millions of years ago, as dryandra fossils have been found in brown coal deposits at Yallourn in Victoria.

Dryandras are often referred to as "honeypots" and are valued by birds, bees and beekeepers for the great quantity of nectar they produce.

Global warming has become a serious issue for the future survival of dryandras, with an estimation that over one quarter of the species will become extinct with a global temperate increase of 0.5%. Six are already endangered.

## Showy Dryandra    *Dryandra formosa*

*Showy Dryandra is the most spectacular of the twelve dryandras growing in the Albany botanical district.*

**FEATURES:** Leaves are arranged around each golden-orange flower like legs on an octopus.

**HABITAT AND DISTRIBUTION:** This species grows wild in the Stirling Ranges and on hills in the vicinity of Albany in Western Australia.

**ECOLOGY:** During the late Palaeocene period, about 56 million years ago, dryandras were also growing in NSW. Fossilised leaves have been found in sediment, identical to the narrow saw toothed leaves of Showy Dryandra.

**FLOWERING PERIOD:** Winter — spring

**HEIGHT:** Up to 4 m

**PROPAGATION:** Seed — requires a limestone base, grows well under cultivation in Perth but not so well in eastern Australia

**STATUS:** Secure — wild populations Protected

**Opposite, top:** Prickly Dryandra (*Dryandra falcata*). **Above:** Showy Dryandra's blooms have some similarities to South Africa's proteas.

# Epacris

## Family: Ericaceae

The *Epacris* genus has 40 species, 35 found in Australia and several others endemic to New Zealand and New Caledonia. The genus *Epacris* comes from the Greek words: "epi" meaning "upon" and "akris" meaning "a hill", referring to the elevated habitat of many of these plants. The Royal Tasmanian Botanical Gardens in Hobart has a collection, which includes all twelve endemic species of *Epacris*. They are known to be under threat for survival in Tasmania's heathlands.

Long flowering *Epacris* species feature masses of tubular stem-clasping flowers in white, pink or red or combinations of colours such as pink and white or red and white. The numerous leaves on these tough small evergreen shrubs are normally very small and often sharply pointed.

About 6% of Australia is heathland habitat in which *Epacris* species thrive from coastal locations to subalpine altitudes no higher than 1000 metres. They can be found beside streams, in swampy heath, woodlands and open forests in Tas, Vic, SA, NSW and Qld but absent from WA and NT.

*Epacris* species are pollinated by several different adult carrion flies and nectar-feeding birds such as the Eastern Spinebill. In alpine heathlands, Montane Heath-blue Butterfly caterpillars feed on host plants, *Epacris breviflora, E. petrophila* and *E. paludosa*.

Germination is known to be improved when seeds have been dormant in darkness for quite some time then subjected to smoke and heat shock from temperatures between 90–110 °C.

## Common Heath   *Epacris impressa*

*Victoria's floral emblem, Common Heath is also known as Pink Heath. French botanist Jacques–Julian Houton de Labillardiere collected Common Heath from Tasmania in 1793, and named it* Epacris impressa *in 1805.*

**FEATURES:** Flower colour varies from perfect pinks to red and white.

**HABITAT AND DISTRIBUTION:** Is widespread on heathlands from sea level to 800 metres in SA, Tas, Vic and NSW.

**ECOLOGY:** In the Northern Hemisphere, Common Heath flowers at Christmas, adding a festive touch and brightening winter gardens, especially in England where it has been cultivated for many years.

**FLOWERING PERIOD:** Autumn — winter — spring

**HEIGHT:** Up to 1 m

**PROPAGATION:** Semi-hardwood cuttings

**STATUS:** Secure — Protected

**Opposite, top:** Fuchsia Heath (*Epacris longiflora*). **Top:** Swamp Heath (*E. paludosa*). **Above, left to right:** Common Heath adds a bright touch to drab winter gardens.

# Eremophila

## Family: Myoporaceae

With names such as Emu Bushes, Desert Fuchsias or Poverty Bushes, and a total of 214 species, *Eremophila* is in the top ten of Australia's genera. Eremophila comes from the Greek words "eremos" meaning "solitude" and "philos" meaning "love of" — referring to the desert loving nature of these plants. Every year in spring an Eremophila Festival is held by Australian Arid Lands Botanic Garden, Port Augusta, showing the largest collection of *Eremophila* species in Australia.

Bell shaped flowers come in white and every colour of the rainbow — red, orange, yellow, green, blue, purple and violet. Many are marked with honey guides to lead insects to the nectar. The foliage of these mainly erect shrubs is generally tough, sometimes wax or hair covered and often resinous. Other clever adaptations to cope with the extremes of Australia's climate include the ability to survive by dropping leaves, not flowering, and being fire tolerant.

*Eremophila* species are widely distributed in all mainland States in low rainfall, arid and semi-arid habitats, mainly in alkaline red sands including dry open plains, mallee and Mulga scrubland, woodland understorey and dry areas subject to flooding. Western Australia has the most species. Eremophilas are absent from bushland in Tasmania. NSW and Qld share *Eremophila debilis* with New Zealand, the only other country in the world to have a species of *Eremophila*.

Over three quarters of the species are insect pollinated and the rest bird pollinated. *E. deserti*, *E. gilesii* and *E. longifolia* are host plants for caterpillars of the butterfly, Rayed Blue (*Candalides heathi*).

The fruit of these plants is safely eaten by emus and bush turkeys, but poisonous to humans. Emu bushes are like a "medicine cabinet" for desert dwelling Aborigines, providing analgesics, antiseptic body washes and cough decongestant. Also smoke from burning foliage is used to strengthen mothers and babies after birth.

## Spotted Fuchsia   *Eremophila maculata*

*Spotted Fuchsia is the most widely cultivated of all Emu Bushes.*

**FEATURES:** Flower colour can vary. Red flowering variety generally has bright red pointed buds opening to a spotted pink and lemon throat advertising the location of nectar.

**HABITAT AND DISTRIBUTION:** Widespread in dry inland areas on alluvial loam, and floodplains of WA, SA, NT, Qld, NSW and Vic. Grows on heavy black soils in the Kimberley region.

**ECOLOGY:** Leaves contain cyanide and can poison animals grazing on the foliage. Aborigines used the foliage as a cold remedy.

**FLOWERING PERIOD:** Winter — spring

**HEIGHT:** Up to 3 m

**PROPAGATION:** Cuttings — good dry area plant, full sun, well drained soil

**STATUS:** Secure

**Clockwise from top:** Spotted Fuchsia
(*Eremophila maculata*); Mackinlay's Emu Bush
(*E. mackinlay*); Emu Bush (*E. glabra*); Berrigan
(*E. longifolia*).

# Eucalyptus & Corymbia
## Family: Myrtaceae

In the world of botany, eucalypts are the signature plant of Australia. To Australians they mean so much — the fragrance or sight of a eucalypt means home. They are held in such high esteem that the House of Representatives in Parliament House, Canberra is decorated with a variety of eucalypt leaf colours.

Australia has two official genera — *Eucalyptus* with over 700 species and *Corymbia* with 113 species.

In Coleraine, Victoria, the Peter Francis Point Arboretum has the largest collection of eucalypts in the Southern Hemisphere.

The tallest flowering plant on Earth is Mountain Ash (*Eucalyptus regnans*) known to grow over 100 m. Bailey's Stringybark (*Eucalyptus baileyana*) has blossoms in sets of seven. Eucalypts always have an odd number of blossoms in a set.

Gum leaves hang down to enable light to reach the forest floor. They turn side on to the sun to prevent sun heating the whole surface of the leaf. A gum leaf has a life of about 2–3 years. Many species have evolved with bright red stems close to the gum blossom offering a perch and directing birds to nectar.

Eucalypts dominate Australia's landscape and grow in every habitat. Half of the population is found in a coastal band 150–600 km wide, from Brisbane, Qld to Spencer Gulf, SA.

Overseas, fifteen *Eucalyptus* species are found in places such as Timor, Indonesia, the Philippines and Papua New Guinea. Five of these fifteen species also grow on Cape York Peninsula and one in the Northern Territory, Australia.

Eucalypts evolved over a long time with an incredible diversity of species, mainly due to fire. It is believed they began 70 million years ago within what is now a World Heritage Site of over one million hectares — the Greater Blue Mountains of NSW.

Globally they are of great importance for reclaiming land, timber, paper, and oil.

**Top:** Blue Gum, Grose Valley, Blue Mountains. **Left:** Eucalypts are believed to have evolved in the Blue Mountains.

# River Red Gum   *Eucalyptus camaldulensis*

The River Red Gum is one of Australia's most stately trees. Aborigines cut bark canoes from the trunks and two famous River Red Gums can be seen in Yarra Park near the Melbourne Cricket Ground.

**Top:** River Red Gums can be found in any waterway, including the Murray River.
**Above:** River Red Gums in Hattah-Kulkyne NP, Vic.

**FEATURES:** River Red Gum's rich russet timber is an extremely durable hardwood. Gnarled old trunks provide numerous hollows for home making by birds such as cockatoos, owls and kookaburras.

**HABITAT AND DISTRIBUTION:** These eucalypts are the most widely distributed in Australia and are found anywhere there is a waterway or an old riverbed. A most important location is along the Murray River and its tributaries.

**ECOLOGY:** The health of River Red Gums in an area of low rainfall depends on being naturally irrigated by floods or by having a high water table in the soil. Egypt grows them for erosion control and bank stabilisation. They are also grown to reduce soil salination.

**FLOWERING PERIOD:** Spring — summer
**HEIGHT:** Up to 15 m

**PROPAGATION:** Seed
**STATUS:** Secure — irrigation and locks along the Murray River create problems for River Red Gums

# Tasmanian Blue Gum · *Eucalyptus globulus*

*Tasmanian Blue Gum was proclaimed Tasmania's floral emblem on 5 December 1962. It is Australia's most important eucalypt ambassador with wide economic use for many countries. It's the main tree grown overseas for eucalyptus oil, with China the largest producer.*

**FEATURES:** Gum blossoms burst from single buds. Tall forest trees are noted for their blue-grey juvenile foliage.

**HABITAT AND DISTRIBUTION:** Grows wild where the annual rainfall is above 600 mm. Native to the east-coast of Tasmania, King and Flinders Island, the Otway Ranges and Wilson's Promontory in Victoria.

**ECOLOGY:** Southern Australia has 450,000 hectares of plantations. Scientists have been studying DNA to improve the wood density, pulp yield, cellulose content and disease resistance of commercial crops.

**FLOWERING PERIOD:** Spring — summer

**HEIGHT:** Up to 60 m

**PROPAGATION:** Seed — too large for garden cultivation

**STATUS:** Secure — there is concern that trees are felled from naturally growing stands

# Salmon Gum · *Eucalyptus salmonophloia*

*Salmon Gum was named by Australia's famous botanist Ferdinand von Mueller. The smooth trunk of this tree is unique with coppery-salmon bark that absolutely glistens.*

**FEATURES:** Cream gum blossom is in clusters and the mature shining green leaves are lance shaped.

**HABITAT AND DISTRIBUTION:** Found in Western Australia growing in loamy soil between Ravensthorpe and Lake Grace. It is the most widespread tree of the wheatbelt and is also found in the goldfields in the south-west.

**ECOLOGY:** Bees produce excellent honey from Salmon Gum. Up until 1913 many very tall Salmon Gums around Ravensthorpe were felled to fuel a copper smelter on Hopetoun Road.

**FLOWERING PERIOD:** Late spring — summer

**HEIGHT:** Up to 25 m

**PROPAGATION:** Seed

**STATUS:** Secure — Protected against felling for timber

# Snow Gum  *Eucalyptus pauciflora*

*Snow Gums make marvellous subjects for the photographer. Twisted trunks have unique character with multi-coloured ornamental bark. Other common names include Cabbage Gum, Weeping Gum and White Sallee.*

**FEATURES:** Produces masses of fluffy white gum blossom.

**HABITAT AND DISTRIBUTION:** Grows on hills, in valleys and the mountain snowfields of alpine areas in Tas, Vic, ACT and NSW.

**ECOLOGY:** Snow Gums are important in preventing soil erosion occurring on mountains.

**FLOWERING PERIOD:** Summer

**HEIGHT:** Up to 15 m

**PROPAGATION:** Packets of seed available — sow seed early spring, germination 3–5 weeks, cool to cold climates

**STATUS:** Secure — common and widespread

# Mottlecah  *Eucalyptus macrocarpa*

*Mottlecah is a mallee gum of Western Australia.*

**FEATURES:** Mottlecah has solitary salmon-pink gum blossoms the size of a tennis ball, the largest of all eucalypts. Leaves, buds, and bark are all a whitish blue-grey.

**HABITAT AND DISTRIBUTION:** Dominates heath in sandy and gravelly soils between Moore River and Hill River and in the wheatbelt of south-west Australia between Corrigan and Wongan Hills.

**ECOLOGY:** The mature leaves on Mottlecah are more like the juvenile leaves seen on many eucalypt saplings. They are tough and have in-built sunscreen to cope with a hot climate.

**FLOWERING PERIOD:** September — November

**HEIGHT:** Up to 5 m

**PROPAGATION:** Seed — not frost resistant, grown as an indoor pot plant in USA

**STATUS:** Secure — some natural habitat has been cleared for wheat farms

# Illyarrie Eucalypt  *Eucalyptus erthrosorys*

**FLOWERING PERIOD:**
Mainly autumn

**HEIGHT:** Up to 10 m

**PROPAGATION:** Packets of seed available — germination in 15 days, protect from frost when young sapling, suited to dry areas

**STATUS:** Secure

*Illyarrie Eucalypt is well known in cultivation.*

**FEATURES:** Each green bud has a red operculum which pops off with the pressure of a multitude of golden stamens. It has a smooth, whitish trunk.

**HABITAT AND DISTRIBUTION:** Found in lime soils on hills near the coast between Murchison and Dongara in Western Australia.

**ECOLOGY:** Provides a great "restaurant" for many creatures, especially during flowering.

---

# Red Flowering Gum  *Corymbia ficifolia*

*Red Flowering Gum is a much loved flowering gum cultivated widely in Australia and overseas. Prior to 1995 this species was* Eucalyptus ficifolia.

**FEATURES:** This bloodwood tree is a prolific bloomer producing gum blossom in shades ranging from a variety of red, orange and pink to cream. Stunted trunks covered by rough bark are often twisted.

**HABITAT AND DISTRIBUTION:** Small pockets of Red Flowering Gum occur naturally to the west of Albany between Denmark and Walpole Western Australia.

**ECOLOGY:** Red Flowering Gum is a very important source of food during the flowering season especially for birds such as lorikeets. Raucous Rainbow Lorikeets visit up to 40 gum blossoms per minute in their search for nectar.

**FLOWERING PERIOD:**
December — February

**HEIGHT:** Up to 12 m

**PROPAGATION:** Packets of seed available — germination 1–3 weeks

**STATUS:** Rare in the wild

# Lemon-scented Gum   *Corymbia citriodora*

*Queensland's Lemon-scented Gum, also known as Spotted Gum, is widely cultivated in Australia and overseas. India, South Africa and Fiji have plantations. Prior to 1995, this species was* Eucalyptus citriodora.

**FEATURES:** Leaves have a fresh lemony fragrance when they are crushed.

**HABITAT AND DISTRIBUTION:** In woodlands from Maryborough to south of Gladstone and further inland.

**ECOLOGY:** The oil citronella is extracted from the leaves to be used in the perfume industry and as a mosquito repellent.

**FLOWERING PERIOD:** Autumn
**HEIGHT:** Up to 40 m
**PROPAGATION:** Seed — wonderful specimen tree
**STATUS:** Secure

# Ghost Gum   *Corymbia aparrerinja*

*Ghost Gum is an Australian icon. Aboriginal artist Albert Namatjira raised global awareness of this magnificent tree with his heart-felt Central Australian landscapes. One of Albert's most famous paintings is "Twin Ghost Gums". Prior to 1995 this species was* Eucalyptus papuana.

**FEATURES:** Stark white powdery bark helps protect the tree by acting as a sunscreen.

**HABITAT AND DISTRIBUTION:** Ghost Gums can be seen growing in red sand or acrobat–like from a crack in red rock at places such as the Devils Marbles, Standley Chasm and Ormiston Gorge in Central Australia.

**ECOLOGY:** Central Australian Aborigines use the gum to help clear up sores and as a leech repellent.

**FLOWERING PERIOD:** Late spring — summer
**HEIGHT:** Up to 20 m
**PROPAGATION:** Seed, wonderful tree for landscaping — caution: is known to drop limbs without warning
**STATUS:** Secure

# Goodenia
## Family: Goodeniaceae

*Goodenia* is one of the largest genera in Australia with 176 endemic species.

There are 181 species of *Goodenia* in the world. This genus was named to honour botanist Rev. Samuel Goodenough (1743–1827), the first treasurer appointed for the Linnaean Society, which was associated with the naming of plants.

The majority of species have quaint frilly yellow flowers, with just a few in white, pink, blue and mauve. A goodenia flower has five petals, two on the top and three lower spreading petals. Plants are trailing or erect perennial herbs or small shrubs to 1.5 m. Leaves vary from glistening green to hairy grey.

Habitats include coastal heathlands, moist sandy soils, mallee, open dry forests and arid inland. The *Goodenia* genus with so many species is widely distributed in all States and Territories of Australia from the coast to the inland.

When wet sclerophyll forests are cleared, Hop Goodenia (*Goodenia ovata*) quickly colonises these large areas. Insect pollinators collect pollen from a minute cup on the tip of the style.

Aborigines understood that the foliage of Hairy Goodenia (*Goodenia lunata*) contained tranquillising properties and they used this as a herbal medicine. They also threw it into billabongs to subdue fish, making them easier to catch.

## Ivy Goodenia   *Goodenia hederacea*

*Ivy Goodenia grows wild trailing its way close to ground throughout bushland.*

**FEATURES:** Leaves are shining green contrasting well with the dainty bright yellow flowers.

**HABITAT AND DISTRIBUTION:** Near coastline and on hills in heath, woodlands, and forests in Qld, NSW, ACT and Vic.

**ECOLOGY:** Ivy Goodenia and all other flowers belonging to the Goodeniaceae family have a unique feature. The style has a vessel with double lips which surrounds the stigma to collect pollen before the flower opens.

**FLOWERING PERIOD:** Spring — summer — autumn

**HEIGHT:** Prostrate with trailing stems sometimes nearly a metre in length

**PROPAGATION:** Division — new roots form where nodes in plants touch the ground

**STATUS:** Secure — common

**Opposite, top:** Hop Goodenia (*Goodenia ovata*). **Top:** Ivy
Goodenia (*G. hederacea*). **Above:** Serrated Goodenia (*G. cycloptera*).

# Gossypium
## Family: Malvaceae

The genus *Gossypium*, thought to have evolved 10–20 million years ago, provides the human race with their most important plant fibre — cotton. Several introduced species of *Gossypium* are used in Australia's cotton industry.

Of about 50 species worldwide, Australia has seventeen, Mexico has eighteen and north-east Africa and Arabia have fourteen.

Flowers are hibiscus-like with five large overlapping petals. Many Australian species are pale pink or mauve with a deep grape or burgundy centre.

Their seeds are covered by dense cotton but Australian species are not thick enough to be commercially viable.

All are drought tolerant perennial shrubs, some spindly and low and others taller and spreading. Most foliage has spotty black oil glands.

Wild growing specimens inhabit sand plains, rocky gullies, dry creek beds and road verges in temperate arid Australia, subtropical–tropical dry monsoon and warm arid areas of Qld, NT and WA. Some of the places they are found in WA include the Pilbara, Kimberleys, Hamersley and Barlee Ranges.

Some of Australia's wild *Gossypium* species are resistant to diseases that infect commercial cotton crops. Scientists are experimenting with chromosomes from wild plants combining them with commercially viable cotton plants to create more effective strains.

Cud chewing animals such as cattle can be poisoned by eating foliage of some *Gossypium* species that contain the toxin gossypol.

## Sturt's Desert Rose     *Gossypium sturtianum*

*The floral emblem of the Northern Territory is Sturt's Desert Rose. Sturt's Desert Rose is named after explorer Captain Charles Sturt.*

**FEATURES:** Flower petals are light mauve with a hint of blue. A crimson red centre surrounds and highlights a pale coloured carpel.

**HABITAT AND DISTRIBUTION:** A widespread plant of arid sandy terrain growing wild in Central Australia in NT, Qld, NSW, SA, and WA.

**ECOLOGY:** Worker ants drag gossypium seeds underground where they eat a fleshly appendage called an elaiosome. This assists seed dispersal and provides storage until time for germination.

**FLOWERING PERIOD:** A year, peaking late winter

**HEIGHT:** Up to 2 m

**PROPAGATION:** Seed and cuttings — suit warm climates, well drained soil

**STATUS:** Secure

**Opposite, top:** Sturt's Desert Rose is the floral emblem of the Northern Territory. **Top and above:** Sturt's Desert Rose in all its colour range.

# Grevillea
## Family: Proteaceae

Australia's third largest genus is *Grevillea*, with most of the 350-plus species endemic to this land. These are the much loved "Spider Flowers" of Australia's flora. Sulewesi and Papua New Guinea have one species each and New Caledonia has three species. *Grevillea* is named to honour a friend of Sir Joseph Banks, Charles F Greville (1749-1809), a founder of the British Horticultural Society and patron of botany. The Australian Garden at Cranbourne Botanic Gardens in Victoria and Mt Annan Botanic Gardens in NSW are providing a custodian role for the genus by growing many species.

Individual flowers, often like cute and colourful curled up snails, group together with natural artistry forming spider, comb, toothbrush, catkin and bottlebrush shapes. All the bird-attracting warm colours of the spectrum are featured and flowers produce copious quantities of sweet nectar. Plants with diverse leaf shapes vary from prostrate ground covers to a range of shrubs and tall trees.

Grevilleas can always be discovered somewhere in Australia from low to high altitudes in coastal, arid and mountainous areas in heath, mallee, red sand and rocky soils.

Nearly half of the *Grevillea* species are considered endangered, rare or threatened. Among other measures taken to ensure their survival, tissue culture is being used by organisations such as Mt Annan Botanic Garden to clone plants, preserving as many threatened species as possible.

Gardeners appreciate the fantastic range of long flowering and hardy grevilleas and cultivars available. Queensland's Mundubbera Grevillea (*Grevillea whiteana*), with deep, cream, flower spikes, is grown extensively in Israel and sold as "Spiderman" for the European cut flower trade.

**Top:** Long-styled Grevillea (*Grevillea longistyla*). **Left:** Rosemary Grevillea.

Silky Oak is always a welcome sight during its spectacular flowering. This tree, the tallest of all grevilleas, is widely cultivated in parks and gardens in Australia and overseas. South Africa has plantations of Grevillea robusta.

**FEATURES:** Flowering spikes are golden-orange and all individual flowers are arranged in a toothbrush shape.

**HABITAT AND DISTRIBUTION:** This indigenous rainforest tree is found in coastal and further inland ranges of NSW and Qld.

**ECOLOGY:** Silky Oaks have a prolific flowering and each tree provides plenty of nectar for birds. *Grevillea robusta* is listed as a weed in the book *Jumping the Garden Fence* by the Worldlife Fund.

**FLOWERING PERIOD:** Spring — summer

**HEIGHT:** 10–30 m sometimes higher

**PROPAGATION:** Seed

**STATUS:** Secure — limited geographical distribution

# Rattlepod Grevillea  *Grevillea stenobotrya*

*During ceremonial dancing, Pitjantjatjara people of Central Australia use the dry seed pods of Rattlepod Grevillea as rhythm rattlers in the same way a maraca is used for percussion.*

**FEATURES:** Pale green buds gradually open into cream flowers forming pointed cylindrical flowerheads. Leaves are like pine needles.

**HABITAT AND DISTRIBUTION:** These inland plants of arid NT, WA, SA, NSW and Qld are found among spinifex on the crests of red sand dunes.

**ECOLOGY:** Aborigines use the fleshy seeds, with a high concentration of mineral nutrients, as a food source.

**FLOWERING PERIOD:** Late winter — spring or after soaking rain

**HEIGHT:** 2–6 m

**PROPAGATION:** Seed — plants are often grafted onto *Grevillea robusta*

**STATUS:** Secure — widespread

# Pink Pokers  *Grevillea petrophiloides*

*Western Australia is the only State where Pink Pokers grow naturally.*

**FEATURES:** Pink flowers form long poker-like blooms. Buds open gradually from the top working their way down to the stem.

**HABITAT AND DISTRIBUTION:** Inland areas of South-West WA support colonies growing in gravel and sandy soils in tall scrub between the Murchison River and Merredin.

**ECOLOGY:** Large introduced bees often rob nectar from this grevillea meant for birds, pushing their way through barriers of hairs designed to deter the smaller native bees.

**FLOWERING PERIOD:** Late winter — spring

**HEIGHT:** 1.5 m sometimes up to 3 m

**PROPAGATION:** Seed — full sun and good drainage required

**STATUS:** Secure — widespread

# Desert Grevillea  *Grevillea juncifolia*

*Desert Grevillea also has another common name, Honeysuckle Grevillea, referring to the marvellous nectar which is enjoyed by Indigenous peoples and birds.*

**FEATURES:** Flame coloured orange and gold blooms. Shrubs have white tomentum covering the stems giving sunscreen protection from harsh sunlight.

**HABITAT AND DISTRIBUTION:** Found in arid inland plains of red sand where Spinifex is also growing and sometimes on the sides of sandhills in WA, NT, Qld, NSW and SA.

**ECOLOGY:** Eastern Warlpiri people of Central Australia used ash from the burnt timber of this plant for healing wounds.

**FLOWERING PERIOD:** Late winter — spring; also flowers well after fire and soaking rain but not during the coldest months of the year

**HEIGHT:** 2–5 m

**PROPAGATION:** Seed — plants are not frost resistant

**STATUS:** Secure — widespread but scattered distribution

# Rosemary Grevillea  *Grevillea rosmarinifolia*

*Rosemary Grevillea has been cultivated in Australian gardens for many years and is widely propagated and grown overseas in places like England and New Zealand.*

**FEATURES:** Shrubs come in a variety of flower colours including pink and cream, red, yellow and light green.

**HABITAT AND DISTRIBUTION:** Some inland mallee and woodland areas of Victoria and New South Wales support the natural growth of Rosemary Grevillea. A low growing form is found in the Little Desert in Vic.

**ECOLOGY:** Crimson Rosellas feast on the ripe fruit (swollen ovaries) of Rosemary Grevillea during autumn.

**FLOWERING PERIOD:** Most of the year but mainly winter — spring

**HEIGHT:** 0.5–2 m

**PROPAGATION:** Cuttings or seed; attractive foliage much like that of the herb Rosemary

**STATUS:** Secure

# Hakea
## Family: Proteaceae

Australia is the only country in the world where 149 species of shrubs and trees in the *Hakea* genus grow wild. These unique plants with diverse ornamental fruits are often referred to as "Corkwoods" due to the incredibly thick, gnarled bark of many species. The *Hakea* genus was named by Schrader in 1797, in honour of Baron Christian Ludwig von Hake, who was a German patron of botany.

Hakea flowers vary in character from tapered spikes (not unlike grevilleas) and clusters to less conspicuous blooms contained within leaf axils. Main colours are white, cream, lemon, yellow, greenish, pink, red and rusty brown.

Mimicry, evolved as a form of defence, is conspicuous in the shapes and textures of the nutty fruit cases. Such cases feature beaks, horns or warts, and imitate other creatures such as frogs and fearsome insects.

Many species have protective needle-like leaves and others have toothed or prickly broad leaves in shapes such as shells, fans, holly and clubs. Flamenco-like, frilly red, green and yellow foliage is displayed by Royal Hakea.

Sandy coastal heath, woodlands, jarrah forests, rocky granite and inland deserts support Hakeas with the largest concentration of about 65% species in south-western Australia. Hakeas are found in every State.

Many of these hardy plants, survivors of environmental extremes, depend on fire for the release of seed and regeneration from lignotubers— water-bearing, swollen rootstock. Needlewood (*Hakea leucoptera*), found in all mainland States, was dug up by Aborigines and explorers for life-saving water.

## Pin-cushion Hakea  *Hakea laurina*

*Pin-cushion Hakea has been widely cultivated for many years. It is valued as a hardy attractive shrub and for its ability to attract birds. Packets of seed are often available in plant nurseries.*

**FEATURES:** Globular flowers have a red pin-cushion centre covered entirely by cream "pins" — stamens.

**HABITAT AND DISTRIBUTION:** Grows in the wild from Israelite Bay in the Great Australian Bight to Albany and up north as far as Narrogin in Western Australia.

**ECOLOGY:** Birds and the honey possum feed on nectar and in return assist with pollination of the species.

**FLOWERING PERIOD:** Autumn — winter

**HEIGHT:** Up to 6 m

**PROPAGATION:** Easy to grow — place seed in moist sandy soil, germinates in 3–6 weeks

**STATUS:** Secure — Protected

**Opposite:** Yellow Hakea (*Hakea nodosa*). **Clockwise from top:** Pin-cushion Hakea; Prickly Hakea (*Hakea amplexicaulis*); Royal Hakea (*Hakea victoria*) from the Ravensthorpe area of south-western Australia.

# Hibbertia

### Family: Dilleniaceae

The world has 115 species belonging to the *Hibbertia* genus with an Australian tally of 110. Other countries with *Hibbertia* species include Papua New Guinea, Fiji, Madagascar and New Caledonia. Featuring Australia's colours of yellow and green, hibbertias are also known as Guinea Flowers. The genus is named after George Hibbert, an 18th-century London merchant, who was a great supporter of botany.

Nearly every species of *Hibbertia* has shining buttercup yellow flowers with the exception of a couple of striking orange species. Each flower is up to 5 cm in diameter with five heart-shaped petals, capable of reflecting ultraviolet radiation. Protective seed coats enable members of this genus to lie dormant until a bushfire promotes germination. Plants range from prostrate spreading, trailing or climbing shrubs to erect rounded or straggly shrubs.

*Hibbertia* species grow in every State of temperate Australia, on sandy plains, open forest and rainforest margins, from the coastline to the mountains. South-west Australia has more than 50% of Australia's species. *Hibbertia glaberrima* has a challenge growing in rocky gorges of Central Australia.

Kangaroos and wallabies graze on the fresh young foliage of some hibbertias. Insect pollination is carried out on several species by the Teddy Bear Bee and Blue Banded Bee, both native bees, using the "buzz" method to spread pollen.

## Climbing Guinea Flower  *Hibbertia scandens*

*Climbing Guinea Flower is often called "Snake Vine" due to its twining nature.*

**FEATURES:** Daffodil-yellow flowers are about 5 cm wide, large for a hibbertia flower.

**HABITAT AND DISTRIBUTION:** A native of eastern Australia on sand dunes, in open forests and edges of rainforests from south-east NSW to north-east Qld.

**ECOLOGY:** This rambling climber has an important role as a soil binder wherever it grows.

**FLOWERING PERIOD:** All year but most prolific in spring and summer

**HEIGHT:** Climbing stems up to 5 m long

**PROPAGATION:** Commonly cultivated from cuttings, quick growing climber

**STATUS:** Secure — widespread, Protected

**Opposite:** *Hibbertia procumbens.*  **Above:** Climbing Guinea Flower
(*Hibbertia scandens*) produces daffodil-like yellow flowers.

# Isopogon
## Family: Proteaceae

*Isopogon* is an endemic genus with 35 species, collectively known as "Drumsticks" due to their bold fruiting cones that look ready to beat a drum. The genus *Isopogon* comes from Greek words "isos" meaning "equal" and "pogon" meaning "a beard" — referring to the hairs on the fruit that are of equal length.

Flowers in shades of cream, yellow, pink and mauve are terminal or found in the upper leaf axils. Long lasting, remarkable cones come in decorative shapes such as golf ball, barrel, small pine cone, acorn and cap. Depending on water supply, the compact flower heads open between October and January but November is the best month for flowering.

These perennial shrubs, often with reddish stems, are mainly low growing with some very prostrate in nature. Some erect species grow to 3–4 m in height.

Leaves come in a variety of shapes and can be prickly.

*Isopogon* species of temperate southern Australia thrive in sandy, laterite and clay soils with a limestone underlay in coastal heaths, dry forest and open woodland. Western Australia has 27 species mainly in the south-west corner and others are found in SA, Vic, NSW and Qld.

Like other genera in the Proteaceae family, *Isopogon* is threatened in Australia by the introduced disease Cinnamon Fungus (*Phytophthora cinnamomi*) which attacks the root system causing plants to collapse and die.

## Broad-leafed Drumsticks    *Isopogon anemonifolius*

*Broad-leafed Drumsticks are hardy to frost and drought.*

**FEATURES:** When in bud, the flowering globular cones look just like drumsticks. Shrubs with uniquely divided leaves are variable, some being almost prostrate, others widely spreading and others upright in nature.

**HABITAT AND DISTRIBUTION:** They grow wild in the ranges and along most of the coastline of NSW and over the border into south Queensland.

**ECOLOGY:** An acidic sandstone soil over a limestone underlay seems to be just the right growing medium for these plants.

**FLOWERING PERIOD:** Spring — summer

**HEIGHT:** Up to 2 m

**PROPAGATION:** Seed and cuttings — needs well drained soil and full sun

**STATUS:** Secure — a common plant

**Opposite, top:** Spreading Cone Bush (*Isopogon divergens*). **Above:** Broad-leaved Drumsticks (*Isopogon anemonifolius*). **Left:** Unlike the Broad-leafed Drumstick, the Coneflower (*Isopogon cuneatus*) is a native of Western Australia.

# Kunzea
### Family: Myrtaceae

*Kunzea* is an Australian genus named in 1828 after Dr Gustave Kunze, German professor of botany and medicine. Of the 42 *Kunzea* species, some have edible fruit and others aromatic foliage, sometimes used by explorers and early settlers to brew tea-like beverages.

During spring and summer, whisker-like stamens protrude from kunzea flowers, creating a very fluffy appearance. Perfumed blooms, resembling callistemons, eucalypts and melaleucas (members of the same family), come in white, cream, yellow, pink, mauve and red.

Kunzeas expel their seeds as soon as they are ripe, instead of storing them in woody capsules as do eucalypts and melaleucas. Plants range in height from ground huggers to shrubs 1–5 m.

*Kunzea* species grow mainly in coastal heath, open forest, granite outcrops and mallee throughout temperate Australia. Yellow Kunzea (*Kunzea muelleri*), grows wild in subalpine and alpine heath, in Vic and NSW.

For thousands of years, Narrindjeri people of the coastal Coorong in South Australia have harvested and eaten apple fragrant Muntries (*Kunzea pomifera*), which are now Australia's fourth most important bushfood crop.

Bandicoots, known to host ticks, shelter under Tick Bush (*Kunzea ambigua*), in southern locations of NSW, Victoria's Wilsons Promontory National Park, Tasmania and the islands of Bass Strait.

## Crimson Kunzea    *Kunzea baxteri*

*Crimson Kunzea has become a widely cultivated plant due to its showy blooms, hardy nature and ability to attract native birds to the garden.*

**FEATURES:** Vibrant red bottlebrush flowers have gold tipped stamens.

**HABITAT AND DISTRIBUTION:** This most attractive shrub grows wild in Western Australia's South-West from Esperance to Israelite Bay.

**ECOLOGY:** Nectar feeding native bees, butterflies and parrots appreciate the flowering of this and other *Kunzea* species and in return assist with pollination.

**FLOWERING PERIOD:** Spring — summer

**HEIGHT:** Up to 3 m

**PROPAGATION:** Seed and cuttings — requires good drainage

**STATUS:** Poorly known within a restricted geographic range; mainly in reserves

**Opposite, top:** Tick Bush has very prominent white stamens and honey-fragrant flowers. **Above:** Crimson Kunzea grows on granite outcrops in Western Australia.

# Lechenaultia

## Family: Goodeniaceae

Australia has twenty endemic species belonging to the genus *Lechenaultia,* which was named after a French botanist, Leschenault de la Tour. He collected specimens in Western Australia when he visited in 1802–1803. Some *Lechenaultia* species boast the richest reds and blues in the botanical world.

Exciting intense flower colours include, amazing flame-like reds, orange, yellow and blue. Blue Lechenaultia (*Lechenaultia biloba*) is one of Western Australia's best known wildflowers with its mass of superb blue flowers. Each flower has two upper petals and three, sometimes frilled, lower petals.

Many plants are prostrate, perennial herbs or small shrubs with the ability to spread by suckering and cloning themselves to propagate new plants.

Western Australia has seventeen species and three others are found in Central Australia and the Northern Territory. Habitats range from sandy heaths, red gravelly soils, woodlands and jarrah forests mainly in South-West Western Australia. North of Perth, in the wheatbelt between the towns of Wubin and Mullewa, unusual specimens of Wreath Lechenaultia (*Lechenaultia macrantha*) have green centres surrounded by red and yellow flowers during spring.

When bushfires sweep over a lechenaultia habitat, dormant seed is activated by chemicals in the smoke and germination commences.

Fresh young roots of *Lechenaultia divaricata* were dug up and eaten by southern Arrernte people of Central Australia. These Aborigines also sourced strong resin from older roots.

## Red Lechenaultia *Lechenaultia formosa*

*Vibrant patches of Red Lechenaultia add great excitement to Western Australia's flora, surprising and delighting many wildflower enthusiasts from all over the world.*

**FEATURES:** This species is famous for lipstick red flowers that may also come in pink, orange, yellow and cream. Shrubs on the southern sandplains and heath regions are erect near the coast but become prostrate in nature further inland.

**HABITAT AND DISTRIBUTION:** It is well known in coastal areas and slightly inland in the eastern Albany district, the Stirling Range and Ravensthorpe region of south-west Australia.

**ECOLOGY:** Growth is more prolific after fierce bushfires.

**FLOWERING PERIOD:** Winter — spring
**HEIGHT:** Up to 50 cm
**PROPAGATION:** Cuttings at any time of the year — seed is difficult
**STATUS:** Secure — common, widespread

**Opposite:** Wreath Lechenaultia. **Above:** Red Lechenaultia also blooms in pink, orange, yellow and cream. **Left:** Yellow Lechenaultia (*Lechenaultia linarioides*) is a prolific flowering, spreading plant of Western Australia.

# Leptospermum
### Family: Myrtaceae

Tea-tree is a colloquial name adopted hundreds of years ago for plants in the *Leptospermum* genus. Aromatic leaves were brewed by early settlers to Australia and New Zealand for a thirst quenching substitute tea. Australia has a tally of 83 of the world's 86 species of *Leptospermum*, some shared with other countries such as Malaysia, Sumatra, Borneo, Java, Sulawesi, the Philippines, Thailand and New Zealand. *Leptospermum* comes from the Greek "leptos" meaning "fine" or "slender" and "sperma" meaning "a seed".

White is the dominant colour of *Leptospermum* species flowers but all shades of pink, rarely red and also mauve are represented. Each flower has five rounded petals and whiskery stamens surrounding a nectar disc centre. These shrubs to small trees, mainly with small leafed closely packed foliage, are frequently aromatic.

Tea-trees, often growing in poor soils, are frequently seen growing on sand dunes, coastal heath, wetlands, swamps, riversides, in open forests and on mountains. The distribution of the tropical *Leptospermum amboinense* extends from Queensland to South-East Asia.

Australia has about 1500 native bees and they love leptospermums for nectar gathering and honey production. Kenya and Guatemala grow Australia's Lemon Scented Tea-tree (*Leptospermum petersonii*) to extract citronella oil which has anti-bacterial and anti-fungal properties and is useful in medicine. Citronella is also used to scent shampoo and other toiletries. Olive Tea-tree (*Leptospermum liversidge*) is an insect repellent.

## Manuka   *Leptospermum scoparium*

*Manuka is the only leptospermum native to both New Zealand and south-east Australia. Manuka is the Maori name for this plant.*

**FEATURES:** Flowers are normally white, sometimes tinged with pink and there are rare red varieties. Manuka grows taller in wet forests. It is a great shelter shrub — especially valued by Ringtail Possums for their nests.

**HABITAT AND DISTRIBUTION:** Manuka is very common in coastal heath in Tas, Vic, NSW and NZ.

**ECOLOGY:** Anti-bacterial properties discovered in the honey have made Manuka world famous. Herbal and medicinal tea was brewed from the leaves of Manuka by Captain Cook and early settlers to Australia and New Zealand.

**FLOWERING PERIOD:** Spring — summer — early autumn

**HEIGHT:** Mainly to 2 m, can reach 6 m in Tasmania's wet forests and 8 m in New Zealand

**PROPAGATION:** Seeds and cuttings — plants don't mind shade

**STATUS:** Secure — common and widespread

**Opposite, top:** Heath Tea-tree (*Leptospermum myrsinoides*). **Clockwise from top left:** Round-leafed Tea-tree (*Leptospermum rotundifolium*) flowers in spring on coastal heath in New South Wales; *Leptospermum spectabile* is only found on banks of Colo River in New South Wales; Manuka is a compact shrub to 2 m high by 2 m wide, suitable for hedging and screening.

# Macadamia
## Family: Proteaceae

Macadamias are one of the world's favourite nuts. The *Macadamia* genus is named after Dr John McAdam, an Australian scientist. The world has nine species, seven in eastern Australia, one in New Caledonia and one in Indonesia. The only two of economic value are Australia's *Macadamia tetraphylla* and *Macadamia integrifolia*.

Macadamias are large evergreen trees with prickly edged, dark green glossy leaves. Long, dangling, creamy white or pinkish flowers are followed by smooth or rough, hard-shelled, marble-shaped, edible nuts ripening late summer to early autumn.

Macadamias grow in rainforest lowlands to an altitude of 400 metres.

*Macadamia tetraphylla*, endemic to subtropical coastal rainforest in Northern NSW and in Queensland's south, is now rare and endangered with a geographic range of less than 100 km.

Australia produces almost half of the world's macadamias with crops in Queensland, Northern NSW and in WA. Hawaii and Central America also have macadamia plantations.

The world's first macadamia power plant operates at Gympie in Queensland. Ergon Energy converts 5000 tonnes of waste shells from nuts per year, into enough power for 1200 homes and factories.

## Macadamia   *Macadamia integrifolia*

*Macadamia produces scrumptious nuts rich in iron, calcium, potassium, magnesium and six vitamins.*

**FEATURES:** The creamy kernels are claimed to have the highest oil content of the world's nuts — 78% mono-unsaturated oil which is cholesterol free.

**HABITAT AND DISTRIBUTION:** *Macadamia integrifolia*, endemic to rainforests of South-East Queensland, is especially known from Mount Bauple north of Gympie.

**ECOLOGY:** Macadamia nuts have tough shells which stop most predators eating them. Luckily humans have solved the problem of shelling these delicious nuts.

**FLOWERING PERIOD:** Winter — spring

**HEIGHT:** 8–20 m

**PROPAGATION:** Grafted seedlings bear nuts when six years of age — need high humidity and no frost

**STATUS:** Vulnerable — used to be common nea Gympie in Queensland

**Opposite, top:** Macadamia kernels are well protected by hard shells. **Clockwise from top:** Macadamias are evergreen trees; A cluster of Australia's favourite nuts; Flowers and unripe nuts.

# Melaleuca
## Family: Myrtaceae

Australia has 220 of the world's 230 melaleucas, known also as paperbarks and honey myrtles. Other countries with melaleucas include New Zealand, Papua New Guinea, Malaysia, Burma and New Caledonia. Species in the *Callistemon* genus are due to be reclassified as melaleucas. Carolus Linnaeus named this genus during the 18th century from the Greek words "melas" meaning "black" and "leucos" meaning "white" (in reference to the bark).

Melaleuca flowers have their stamens in bundles of five and come in every colour of the rainbow except blue. Most species have soft fluffy "bottlebrushes" made up of many tiny flowers and their nectar is a great attraction for birds and bees. Many species have trunks covered by several layers of thin papery cork which acts as insulation and sunscreen. Trees, adapted to a habitat with a wet season or regular flooding, store air inside their trunks enabling them to breathe when submerged.

Australia has 90,501 km$^2$ of melaleuca forests and woodlands. Western Australia has at least 100 species. Some trees are long living, known to be well over a hundred years of age. Many species are water-loving swamp dwellers.

Aborigines have a myriad of uses for paperbark, including use as a blanket, mattress or disposable nappy. It can also be used to wrap around a broken limb as a splint, for food wrapping or to waterproof a hole in a canoe. A diversity of applications including use as containers make paperbark an ingenious tool for Indigenous Australians.

Threats include drainage of swamplands and the building of floodgates.

## Narrow-leafed Paperbark    *Melaleuca linariifolia*

*Many years ago Narrow-leafed Paperbark was introduced to England where it is now widely cultivated as "Snow-in-Summer".*

**FEATURES:** Masses of fluffy white flowers make the trees look as though they have been dusted with snow. Trunks have papery bark.

**HABITAT AND DISTRIBUTION:** These water loving trees are often encountered on the coast and nearby ranges where they grow beside rivers and swamps.

**ECOLOGY:** Birds in search of insects frequent these trees during the flowering season.

**FLOWERING PERIOD:** Late spring — early summer

**HEIGHT:** Up to 10 m

**PROPAGATION:** Seed or cuttings — dwarf cultivars are available from nurseries with names such as Snowstorm and Snowflake

**STATUS:** Secure

**Above:** Narrow-leafed Paperbark, is aptly referred to as "Snow-in-Summer" due to its characteristic white flowers.

# Broad-leaved Paperbark *Melaleuca quinquenervia*

*Broad-leaved Paperbark is native to Australia, Papua New Guinea, Indonesia and New Caledonia.*

**FEATURES:** Broad-leaved Paperbark is a tallish tree with a papery bark trunk. It has bird and insect attracting cream or white bottlebrush blooms.

**HABITAT AND DISTRIBUTION:** In Australia it grows beside rivers and in swampy coastal areas. On the east coast of Australia it is found from Cape York right down to Botany Bay in NSW.

**ECOLOGY:** Broad-leaved Paperbark is a host plant for Ghost Moths. Explorers and early settlers valued this tree for brewing a lemon-flavoured tea from the leaves.

**FLOWERING PERIOD:** Autumn — winter

**HEIGHT:** Mainly up to 12 m but sometimes reaches 25 m

**PROPAGATION:** Seed or cuttings — tolerant of bad drainage

**STATUS:** Secure — common

# Claw Honey Myrtle *Melaleuca pulchella*

*Claw Honey Myrtle can be successfully grown in temperate areas.*

**FEATURES:** The mauve flowers are unique for melaleucas being the largest individual flower of all species. The common name comes from the appearance of the large claw-like, incurved feathered stamens.

**HABITAT AND DISTRIBUTION:** Restricted to Western Australia coastal sandplains between Hopetoun and Israelite Bay.

**ECOLOGY:** Claw Honey Myrtle and other melaleuca blossoms evolved for a range of pollinators including birds, mammals, native bees, wasps and butterflies.

**FLOWERING PERIOD:** Spring — summer

**HEIGHT:** Up to 2 m

**PROPAGATION:** Seed or cuttings — sunny or slightly shaded position

**STATUS:** Secure

# Graceful Honey Myrtle  *Melaleuca radula*

**FLOWERING PERIOD:**
September — November

**HEIGHT:** 1–2 m

**PROPAGATION:** Seed
or cuttings — sunny
position

**STATUS:** Secure
— widespread

*Graceful Honey Myrtle grows wild in Western Australia's famous South-West botanical area.*

**FEATURES:** Blooms are mauve to magenta and a rare white variety exists. It has tough narrow leaves and very effective roots that can search for water through cracks in rocks.

**HABITAT AND DISTRIBUTION:** Found in Western Australia on gravelly heath and in granite outcrops from the Murchison River to Perth and inland to Southern Cross.

**ECOLOGY:** Rock dwelling Graceful Honey Myrtle has leaves and roots adapted for survival during the intense heat of summer.

---

# Cork Bark Honey Myrtle  *Melaleuca suberosa*

*Cork Bark Honey Myrtle is a very small shrub with some unusual features.*

**FEATURES:** Rose coloured blooms with gold tipped stamens appear to burst from the thick, corky bark.

**HABITAT AND DISTRIBUTION:** It grows wild on Western Australia's southern coastal sandheaths from Albany to Israelite Bay.

**ECOLOGY:** The older wood on stems has an extremely thick coating of roughly textured cork. This is designed to protect the plant from extremes in temperature and also to deter predators.

**FLOWERING PERIOD:**
Spring

**HEIGHT:** Up to 70 cm

**PROPAGATION:** Seed or cuttings — hardy, needs full sun

**STATUS:** Secure

# Prostanthera
## Family: Lamiaceae

Fresh fragrances of Australia's "Mint Bushes" permeate bushland adding character to this nation's unique botanical collection. Lavender, rosemary and culinary mints share the same family, Lamiaceae. The *Prostanthera* genus is endemic to Australia, with approximately 100 species.

Sprays of tubular flowers in every imaginable shade of mauve, blue, white and sometimes red, pink, yellow or green, add to the sensual beauty of these aromatic shrubs or small trees. Throats of some species are marked with spots or stripes for honey guides. At Christmas time, the Victorian Christmas Bush (*Prostanthera lasianthos*), with whitish lilac flowers, adds a festive touch to forests in Vic, Tas, NSW, ACT and Qld.

Prostantheras grow in a wide range of habitats including along riverbanks, in damp gullies, on rocky hillsides, in shaded cool temperate forests, subalpine heath, mallee and inland desert. They are represented in every State of Australia.

Many species of *Prostanthera* provide food and shelter as host plants for the caterpillars of hepialid moths.

Leaves were used as aromatic medicines by Aborigines and pioneers, who inhaled the vapour from crushed leaves to treat colds and influenza.

# Mint Bush   *Prostanthera discolor*

*It is estimated that the population of this rare Mint Bush is only 110 plants in the wild.*

**FEATURES:** Flowers have the mauve-violet signature colouring of many species of Mint Bush. Foliage has a strong and pleasing mint aroma.

**HABITAT AND DISTRIBUTION:** Found on well drained slopes beside creeks and in open forest. Small populations are known from a few localities in the Central Western Slopes Botanical Division of NSW in the Rylstone and Muswellbrook Shires.

**ECOLOGY:** Plants have a life span of only 10–15 years and are very fire sensitive. At Wollemi National Park a recovery plan limits controlled burning in known habitats. Flowers are likely to be pollinated by insects.

**FLOWERING PERIOD:** September — October

**HEIGHT:** 0.6–3 m

**PROPAGATION:** Rare in cultivation; seed has poor viability

**STATUS:** Vulnerable — at risk of extinction within 20–50 years

**Opposite:** Victorian Christmas Bush flowers at Christmas time. **Above:** The rare *Prostanthera discolor* — some botanic gardens propagate these plants to ensure their survival.

# Ptilotus
## Family: Amaranthaceae

Australia has 100 endemic species belonging to the *Ptilotus* genus with only one other species in another country. Collectively these plants are known as mulla mullas.

A multitude of tiny flowers, each with five hairy petals, combine to make fluffy individual blooms in many shapes including pussy tails, fox-tails, feather dusters and pom-poms. A soft colour range includes white, cream, lemon, pale green, silver, grey, pink, mauve and red. Being ephemeral in nature these perennial herbs respond to soaking rains, transforming arid patches into colourful carpets.

*Ptilotus* species are indigenous plants from a variety of habitats, including arid areas, open plains and woodlands in every mainland State. Tasmania has the very attractive Pussy Tails (*Ptilotus spathulatus*) growing in dry grassy localities.

In Central Australia, several different species grow in the MacDonnell Ranges in very rocky ground.

Aborigines lined cradle-sized coolamons with mulla mullas to create soft bedding for their babies. An extract from mulla mullas is now used in medical science to help treat skin cancer. Attractive species are valued in the horticultural trade for their frost and drought tolerance and striking blooms are also important in the cut flower industry.

## Tall Mulla Mulla    *Ptilotus exaltatus*

*Tall Mulla Mulla sometimes called "Lamb's Tail", is a plant much sought after by the floral industry. In Germany it is frequently grown as a pot plant.*

**FEATURES:** Fluffy, mauve-pink blooms are shaped like feather dusters.

**HABITAT AND DISTRIBUTION:** Tall Mulla Mulla grows in the wild in dry areas of all mainland States. In the inland hills and ranges it grows on gravelly slopes.

**ECOLOGY:** It is a male sex totem for the Warlpiri people of Central Australia.

**FLOWERING PERIOD:** Mainly winter — spring

**HEIGHT:** Up to 60 cm

**PROPAGATION:** Poor germination from seed — try root cuttings, attractive pot plant

**STATUS:** Secure, very common — some States require a licence to pick from the wild

**Opposite, top:** Field of Mulla Mulla wildflowers. **Above:** Masses of Tall Mulla Mulla (*Ptilotus exaltatus*) provide an exciting contrast to the ochre coloured substrates of the inland.

# Rhododendron
## Family: Ericaceae

*Rhododendron* is a large world genus, with 850 species. It includes the popular garden shrubs known as azaleas. For many years, Australia only had one official species, Native Rhododendron (*Rhododendron lochiae*). However, in recent years another member, *Rhododendron notiale* has been discovered.

The main difference between the two Australian species, both of which have brilliant trumpet shaped waxy red flowers, is that the flower tube of *R. lochiae* is straight and *R. notiale* is curved.

Plants are low spreading shrubs with dark green, glossy-oval leaves.

Australia's endemic rhododendrons need high humidity and high rainfall and consequently have a restricted distribution in Queensland's Wet Tropics World Heritage Area. Here they receive good drainage, good light and grow well in semi-shaded aspects protected from hot sun.

Some rhododendrons are found growing on rainforest trees as epiphytes, taking their moisture and nutrients from the air. They are anchored to, but do not feed from the host tree.

A specimen of the Native Rhododendron (*R. lochiae*) was first cultivated at Kew Gardens in 1939.

## Native Rhododendron    *Rhododendron lochiae*

*Native Rhododendron is regarded as an extremely unique botanical asset to Australia due to the rarity of Rhododendron species in this land.*

**FEATURES:** Shrubs are cliff dwellers, sending their fine, hair-like roots into rock crevices.

**HABITAT AND DISTRIBUTION:** They can be found at high altitudes in the coastal granite mountain chain of Bellenden Ker. One location is Mount Lewis Forest Reserve.

**ECOLOGY:** Native Rhododendron belongs to Ericaceae, the same family as *Epacris*, a heath genus.

**FLOWERING PERIOD:** Spring — summer

**HEIGHT:** 0.8–1.2 m

**PROPAGATION:** Cuttings or seeds — plants need a mild shady position with protection from frost, slow growing

**STATUS:** Rare

**Opposite and above:** The Native Rhododendron (*Rhododendron lochiae*) produces clusters of up to six flowers per cluster.

# Santalum
## Family: Santalaceae

Australia has six of the world's 25 species of *Santalum* often called "Sandlewoods" due to their fragrant timber. In Australia, these trees have widely become known as quandongs, from an Aboriginal name given by the Wiradjuri people of south-west NSW.

These evergreen trees have clusters of tiny cream to soft green flowers (some scented) and are amazing survivors in a harsh climate with periods of drought.

All *Santalum* species have edible fruit with colours including the bright red of Wild Peach (*Santalum acuminatum*) and the blue fruit of Northern Sandlewood (*Santalum lanceolatum*). Northern Sandlewood or Plum Bush is widespread in desert and tropical areas of northern Australia.

Salt-tolerant Bitter Quandong (*Santalum murrayanum*) is found in arid areas in WA and near the Murray River in Northern Victoria and South Australia.

*Santalum* species are semi-parasites and early survival depends on an association with deep-rooted perennials to gain nutrients. Once established this relationship often ceases. Emus use the round fruit stones to grind contents of their stomachs and feral camels graze heavily on the fruit. In the past, natural stands of Sandlewood (*Santalum spicatum*) in WA and SA were severely exploited to supply China and India with fragrant wood for joss sticks.

## Quandong or Wild Peach    *Santalum acuminatum*

*Huge plantations of Quandong or Wild Peach have been established for Australia's thriving bushfood industry, to provide fruit for jams, relishes, sauces and desserts.*

**FEATURES:** The marble-shaped fruit is a spectacular glowing red with tasty, pale yellow flesh covering crinkled, round stones.

**HABITAT AND DISTRIBUTION:** Wild plants of Quandong or Wild Peach are found in almost all of Australia's arid red sandy habitats including spinifex plains, mallee, Mulga and near waterways.

**ECOLOGY:** For thousands of years, Aborigines in arid areas have eaten the fresh quandong fruits, and dried their flesh to pound into powder for cake making.

**FLOWERING PERIOD:** Mainly spring — summe

**HEIGHT:** Up to 5 m

**PROPAGATION:** Remov shell from kernels, soak in water with a little bleach then plant with *Acacia* or *Cassia* species seeds (host plants)

**STATUS:** Vulnerable — risk of vanishing from the wild within 50 years

**Opposite:** Quandong fruit provides a tasty treat, rich in vitamin C. **Above:** Desert Quandong (*Santalum acuminatum*). **Right:** Buds, fruit and kernels of Quandong.

# Swainsona

## Family: Fabaceae

*Swainsona* has approximately 85 species with all but one endemic to Australia. Plants in this genus are sometimes called "Vetches". The species name honours Isaac Swainson, a 19th-century private gardener who lived at Twickenham in London.

Colours of these pea flowers include purple, mauve, blue, white, pink, yellow, orange brown and blood red. Flowering is followed by swollen pods containing the seed. Plants range from prostrate, short-lived ephemerals, annuals and perennials to small shrubs. Feather-shaped pinnate leaves are either smooth or covered in woolly tomentum.

Central Australia has at least seventeen species existing in sandy desert loams on a very low rainfall between 125–250 mm. In arid areas, patches of swainsona thrive on inter-dune swales and are often seen by travellers where plants have taken advantage of roadside run-off. Other *Swainsona* species are found in coastal, woodland, mallee and floodplain habitats in Western Australia, Victoria, South Australia, New South Wales and Queensland.

Bird pollination is unusual as most are insect pollinated. Mycorrhizal fungi have a vital symbiotic relationship with *Swainsona* species and, being legumes, nitrogen fixing bacteria inhabit the nodules of their root systems. Cattle have been known to suffer from poisoning when they have grazed on some species.

## Sturt's Desert Pea    *Swainsona formosa*

*Australia's much admired, flamboyant Sturt's Desert Pea is South Australia's floral emblem. The common name honours explorer Captain Charles Sturt, who collected several of these flowers near Coopers Creek in 1845.*

**FEATURES:** Aboriginal names include "malu" (kangaroo eyes) and "meekyluka" (flowers of the blood), perfect descriptions for these blood red flowers. The big black kangaroo eye-like markings are only present on mature flowers.

**HABITAT AND DISTRIBUTION:** Sturt's Desert Pea flourishes after heavy rain, clothing wide patches of red desert.

**ECOLOGY:** Sturt's Desert Pea is a host plant for the caterpillar of the Long-tailed Pea-blue Butterfly. Honeyeaters also interact with this flower causing cross pollination in their search for nectar.

**FLOWERING PERIOD:** July — March

**HEIGHT:** Prostrate to 20 cr

**PROPAGATION:** Prepare seed by soaking it in near boiling water, then plant in moist sandy soil in a pot or rockery in full sun

**STATUS:** Secure — Protected; must not be picked from wild habitats

**Opposite:** An expanse of Sturt's Desert Pea in full bloom.  **Top, left to right:** *Swainsona oroboides; S. canescens;* A rare pink variant of *S. formosa*.  **Above:** Mature red flowers of Sturt's Desert Pea (*S. formosa*).

# Telopea
## Family: Proteaceae

The genus *Telopea* is confined to Australia. It has five species, all called waratahs. *Telopea* is well named, coming from the Greek word "telopos" which means "seen from afar". Early settlers to Port Jackson in Australia adopted the local Aboriginal name "waratah" which means "tree with red flowers".

Each bloom is comprised of up to 250 flowers, mainly in red. There are unusual white and yellow variants. Species vary from shrubs about one to two metres to trees up to seven metres high.

*Telopea* species can be found on the edge of cool rainforests and dry open woodland. They occur in Tasmania, Victoria and New South Wales from sea level up to 1000 metres. Many of Sydney Basin's national parks have endemic waratahs.

Pollination of waratahs is supported by nectar seeking small marsupials and honeyeaters. Nectar was also sucked from blooms by Aborigines in south-east Australia.

The cut flower industry prizes waratahs for their stunning long-lasting blooms and plantations have been established in Australia (Bilpin Waratah Farm in Bilpin, NSW, has over 2500 plants). Other countries to grow waratahs, include South Africa, Israel, Hawaii and New Zealand.

## NSW Waratah    *Telopea speciosissima*

*The magnificent NSW Waratah achieved "star" status when declared as New South Wales' floral emblem, on 24 October 1962.*

**FEATURES:** This species has incredible showcase globe-shaped flower heads coloured bright red. A rare white form was found in NSW southern highlands and is now marketed as Wirrimbirra White Waratah.

**HABITAT AND DISTRIBUTION:** It is found from sea level to 1000 metres — in the high rainfall of the Hawkesbury sandstone area, in south coast bushland, the Blue Mountains and around Sydney.

**ECOLOGY:** Plants have evolved with tough leaves covered by cutin, a raincoat-like veneer, which protects against moisture loss and makes them frost resistant.

**FLOWERING PERIOD:**
Spring — early summer

**HEIGHT:** Up to 3 m

**PROPAGATION:**
Winged seeds take about three weeks to germinate

**STATUS:** Secure — Protected; wild harvest is illegal

**Opposite:** The amazing colour of a Wirrimbirra White Waratah.
**Top and right:** NSW Waratah is fairly widespread on the Central Coast and adjoining mountains of NSW. **Above:** Tasmanian Waratah (*Telopea truncata*).

# Verticordia
### Family: Myrtaceae

*Verticordia* is an Australian genus with 101 species frequently referred to as feather flowers. This festive flora sets the bush ablaze with explosions of cheerful colour in late spring. When the botanist, de Candolle, named this genus he chose *Verticordia*, from Latin words meaning "to turn the heart" because he was so impressed with these whimsical flowers. Kings Park in Perth has a display of many *Verticordia* species growing along Federation Walkway.

Feathery, fringed sepals add to the appeal of these flowers, which come in the warmest "firelight" colours of gold, yellow, orange, red, pink and silvery white. Blue is absent. Flowers are massed either as spikes or as compact clusters. Anthers have claw-like appendages. Plants are prostrate, densely rounded or straggly shrubs up to 2.5 m high. Species of tropical Australia are taller.

Feather flowers are prominent in South-West Western Australia on sandplains, heath and granite outcrops in remnant native vegetation. Locations include the Upland Plain of northern Ravensthorpe and Murchison botanical areas. Plumed Feather Flower (*V. plumosa*), with dense clusters of pink scented flowers, occurs naturally in all regions of south-west Australia and is the most well-known feather flower in cultivation. Two species are common in the north-west on sand dunes between Onslow and Carnarvon, tropical NT and northern Qld. They are also found in SA.

Some Australian native bees are entirely dependent on the existence of some species as their food source. Feather flowers have been picked from the wild for the floristry trade and fortunately this practice is decreasing due to the cultivation of suitable ornamental species.

## Common Yellow Feather Flower
### *Verticordia chrysantha*

*Merredin in Western Australia has selected this beautiful feather flower as the town's floral emblem.*

**FEATURES:** Each fringed golden-yellow flower is like a little rayed sun.

**HABITAT AND DISTRIBUTION:** It occurs on the southern sandplains in Western Australia where there is winter rainfall. Prolific between Lake Grace and Lake King on low sandheath.

**ECOLOGY:** It is an important food source for birds, butterflies and other insects, often glistening with nectar.

**FLOWERING PERIOD:** Late spring — summer

**HEIGHT:** Up to 1 m

**PROPAGATION:** Cutting — full sun, add compost well drained position, mulch well

**STATUS:** Secure — common and Protected

**Opposite, top:** Plumed Feather Flowers bring a festive touch to any occasion. **Above:** The Common Yellow Feather Flower promotes a cheery disposition. **Left:** Tropical Feather Flower (*Verticorida verticillata*) is a shrub with sweetly fragrant flowers.

# Wahlenbergia
## Family: Campanulaceae

Wild Bluebells are a much loved feature of Australia's bush, enhancing natural vegetation with patches of blue. Australia has 26 of the world's 200 Bluebells belonging to the *Wahlenbergia* genus. Other countries include New Zealand, Europe, southern China, the Himalayas, Japan, India, Madagascar, South Africa, and South America. *Wahlenbergia* is named to honour Georg Göran Wahlenberg (1780–1831) Professor of Botany at Uppsala, Sweden.

Dainty bell shaped flowers with five petals come in many shades of blue and white. Plants are annual or perennial herbs, with leaves concentrated at the base of stems. Short lived perennials have fleshy taproots. Long lived perennials form dense trailing tufts to about 50 cm high and are self propagating by sending out underground rhizomes.

All States of Australia have some *Wahlenbergia* species found in native grasslands, beside roadsides and watercourses, in red desert sands, in woodlands and alpine locations.

Wahlenbergia seed is dispersed by wind. Plants have the ability to monitor release of seed by opening seed capsules in dry weather and closing again if it rains. Plants are known to colonise natural bushland sites that have been disturbed.

## Royal Bluebell  *Wahlenbergia gloriosa*

*The Australian Capital Territory's floral emblem is the Royal Bluebell, declared on 26 May 1982.*

**FEATURES:** Flowers are violet-blue bells. Plants cope well during cold winters with frost and sometimes snow.

**HABITAT AND DISTRIBUTION:** This woodland, subalpine plant will only grow in the wild at altitudes above 1300 m in ACT, NSW and Vic.

**ECOLOGY:** Masarine wasps, bees, butterflies, moths and ground feeding birds all forage for nectar in Bluebell flowers.

**FLOWERING PERIOD:** Late spring — summer

**HEIGHT:** Up to 40 cm

**PROPAGATION:** Seed, cuttings or divide underground rhizomes — ground cover

**STATUS:** Secure — Protected; plants cannot be removed from their natural habitat

**Opposite, top:** *Wahlenbergia speciosa*. **Top:** Royal Bluebell, ACT's floral emblem is restricted to the alpine and subalpine areas of the ACT, south-eastern NSW and eastern Vic. **Above, left and right:** Native Bluebells, *Wahlenbergia tumidifructa*.

# Xanthorrhoea

## Family: Xanthorrhoeaceae

*Xanthorrhoea* is uniquely Australian — a living botanical legacy from over 200 million years ago, with 28 endemic species. Wherever these plants (known as grass-trees) grow in the wild, their features dominate adding charisma to the Australian landscape. *Xanthorrhoea* comes from the Greek words "Xanthos" for yellow and "rheo" meaning "to flow" (refers to the resin in the plants).

Thousands of tiny, cream, six petalled flowers adorn the flowering spikes that emerge after summer fires and grow nearly 3 cm per day. A grassy skirt surrounds each ancient trunk. A grass-tree with a trunk measuring 3 m high would be at least 300 years of age. The trunkless species from Qld and NSW, Coastal Grass-tree (*Xanthorrhoea macronema*), has wiry 1.5 m stems topped with small cream spikes.

Some species of grass-tree are found in every State of Australia. Habitats range from coastal heath, swamps and plains to hillside slopes. Desert Grass-tree (*Xanthorrhoea thorntonii*) is only found in a few restricted inland locations such as Gosse's Bluff and Kings Canyon in Central Australia.

These plants are veteran survivors, thriving despite numerous wild bushfires and withstanding severe drought.

Grass-trees provide nectar and high energy food for Aborigines. Their other uses include "knife-like" leaves to cut meat, flower stalks for spears or torches and hard setting resin for tool making.

## Austral Grass-tree  *Xanthorrhoea australis*

*The Austral Grass-tree is a veteran of the bush in eastern Australia, with the taller ones boasting centuries of living.*

**FEATURES:** Flowering spikes, kangaroo tail-like, are clothed with tightly packed minute cream flowers. Grassy skirts surround each spike.

**HABITAT AND DISTRIBUTION:** Widespread in eastern Australia's bush including SA, Vic, Tas, ACT and NSW.

**ECOLOGY:** Over 100 vertebrates and 315 invertebrates gain food and shelter from grass-trees.

**FLOWERING PERIOD:** Spring — summer especially following a bushfire

**HEIGHT:** Normally up to 3 m, some up to 7 m (700 years old)

**PROPAGATION:** Seed germinates within 3–6 weeks — sunny position, drought resistant

**STATUS:** Secure — Protected; current threats include illegal removal by humans and the plant disease, Cinnamon Fungus, which attacks roots causing collapse and death

**Opposite:** A Desert Grass-tree. **Clockwise from top:** Austral Grass-trees; The taller the Austral Grass-tree, the older it is; Austral Grass-tree; Up, close and personal with an Austral Grass-tree; Coastal Grass-tree.

# Xerochrysum

## Family: Asteraceae

Australia has seven species belonging to the "everlasting daisy" genus *Xerochrysum*. During 1990, Tzvelev, a Russian botanist, published this genus and it wasn't until 2002 that existing *Bracteantha* species in Australia were officially changed to *Xerochrysum*. The genus comes from the Greek "xeros" meaning "dry" and "chrysos" meaning "golden", referring to the papery bracts surrounding the centre.

These wild everlasting daisies come in yellow, orange and white. Some white ones are tinged with pale pink. Numerous pointed papery bracts surround the centre made up of scores of tiny florets. The style in each floret is forked at the end.

Each daisy produces many bullet-shaped seeds with the ability to remain dormant until conditions are right for germination.

Plant forms range from low and spreading to erect annual or perennial herbs.

Species of *Xerochrysum* can be found in sandy, limestone and rocky soils in heath, grasslands and open forests from the coast to the arid interior. Orange Everlasting (*Xerochrysum subundulata*) is found in alpine fields of Vic, Tas and NSW.

Bees, butterflies and ants visit the flowers assisting in the pollination process. The tiny pollen grains are so resistant to decomposition, that it is possible for pollen to be preserved for thousands of years.

## Golden Everlasting *Xerochrysum bracteatum*

*Golden Everlasting is most likely the best known everlasting daisy in the world. Plant breeders have been experimenting with this plant for over one hundred years and exciting cultivars have been developed with an amazing range of colours.*

**FEATURES:** Golden Everlasting has shining stiff papery bracts. Most flowers are bright yellow and white forms exist. An extremely variable annual or perennial plant with some subspecies.

**HABITAT AND DISTRIBUTION:** Grows wild in every State of Australia from the mountains to the sea and also in arid areas. It is the only everlasting daisy growing in the tropical top end of Australia.

**ECOLOGY:** Many different butterflies are attracted to these highly visual and fragrant paper daisies, especially the Painted Lady Butterfly, Cabbage Butterfly and occasionally the Monarch Butterfly.

**FLOWERING PERIOD:** Variable depending on location

**HEIGHT:** 0.2–1.5 m

**PROPAGATION:** Readily by seed but can be grown from cuttings

**STATUS:** Secure — common and widespread

**Opposite:** A Golden Everlasting bloom *(Xerochrysum bracteatum)*. **Clockwise from top:** Golden Everlasting *(X. bracteatum)*; Sticky Everlasting *(X. viscosum)*; Golden Everlasting *(X. bracteatum)*; White form of *X. bracteatum* growing in the limestone Dongara area of WA.

# Glossary

**ALIEN** Vegetation foreign to the land.

**ALKALINE** A soil that is not acidic, and contains calcium e.g. limestone.

**ANNUAL** Completing a life cycle in one year.

**ANTHER** Contains the pollen and is located at the top of the stamen.

**AROMATIC** A plant emitting an odour — often with oil glands in the foliage.

**AXIL** The upper angle between a leaf and a stem.

**BIODIVERSITY** The relationship between and variety of life forms within an ecosystem.

**BLOOM** Flower blossom.

**BOTANIST** A person who has made a serious study of plants.

**BOTANY** The study of plants.

**BRACT** A modified leaf at the base of flowers or other structures.

**CLONE** Propagating plants from genetically identical material.

**COLONISE** A species of plant successfully establishing life in an area.

**COMPOUND** A compound inflorescence (bloom) is composed of many tiny individual flowers.

**DIOECIOUS** Species with separate female and male plants.

**ECOLOGY** The relationships living things have with each other and with the environment.

**ELAIOSOMES** Fleshy appendages on a seed.

**ENDANGERED** At serious risk of vanishing from wild habitats within 10–20 years.

**ENDEMIC** Native to and restricted to a country or area.

**EPHEMERAL** Short lived annual that avoids germination until there is enough rain to sustain life.

**EPIPHYTE** A plant attached and growing on another plant. It is not a parasite and can exist from collecting nutrients from the air and water.

**EVERGREEN** Does not shed leaves in autumn like deciduous trees.

**EVOLUTION** A process of genetic development and adaptation to the environment.

**EXTINCT** No longer with a living representative in the world.

**FERAL** An exotic plant introduced from another country that has become wild.

**FLORA** Plants of a country, region or habitat.

**FLORET** One of many individual tiny flowers making up a composite head.

**FLOWER** Reproductive part of a plant mostly with both male and female organs.

**GENERA** Plural of genus, referring to subdivisions within a family.

**GENUS** A group of related species with similar characteristics.

**HERBICIDE** A toxic substance used to kill unwanted vegetation.

**ICONIC** Describes well-known plants with very special significance.

**INDIGENOUS** Native or belonging naturally to a region or country.

**INFUSION** Steeping foliage in water.

**LABELLUM** An orchid's lower lip-like petal.

**LANCE** A weapon shape — referring to a leaf tapered at each end.

**LEGUME** A plant such as the *Acacia* species producing a fruit pod that splits into two to release the seeds.

**LIGNOTUBER** Dormant buds in a swelling at the base of a stem can activate new growth especially after a bushfire, e.g. Myrtaceae and Proteaceae families.

**LIMESTONE** A sedimentary rock composed mainly of calcium carbonate.

**LITHOPHYTE** Plants growing on or from a rock or cliff.

**MALLEE** Low growing multi-stemmed eucalypts.

**NECTAR** A sugary fluid manufactured by plants to attract pollinators.

**OPERCULUM** A cap on the bud, e.g. eucalypt buds.

**OVARY** Female reproductive organ containing ovules which are fertilised by pollen to become seed.

**PERENNIAL** Herbaceous plant that dies down each year growing again for at least three more years.

**PETALS** Floral appendages forming the corolla.

**PHEROMONE** Chemical released by an organism to gain a response from another organism.

**PHYLLODE** A flat tough stalk that acts like a leaf.

**PIGMENT** Natural colouring in the tissue of a plant.

**POLLEN** Minute yellow grains released from the male's anther to fertilise the ovules in the female plant's ovary.

**POLLINATION** The act of aiding the fertilisation of a plant.

**PREDATOR** An insect, bird or animal that eats the plant.

**PROSTRATE** Growing close to the ground often with spreading or trailing foliage.

**PROTEOID** Describes the fine mass of water-seeking roots of plants in the Proteaceae family.

**PSEUDOBULBS** An orchid's swollen stem that bears leaves.

**RARE** Restricted distribution or uncommon over a wide area.

**RESINOUS** Sticky aromatic substance secreted from trees and plants, e.g. gum from a eucalypt or pine.

**RHIZOME** Creeping underground root with ability to self propagate.

**SALINITY** The concentration of salts in water or soil.

**SANDSTONE** Sedimentary rock composed of grains of sand.

**SCARIFY** To scratch the surface of the seed.

**SCLEROPHYLL** A plant with tough stiff leaves such as a eucalypt.

**SEPALS** Floral parts that form an outer ring (whorl) around the stem forming a calyx.

**SHRUB** A woody plant smaller than a tree, often growing in undergrowth.

**SPECIES** Individual within a group (genus) having similar genetic features.

**SPINIFEX** Is a tough grass growing over one fifth of Australia's continent.

**STAMEN** The male part of a flower made of a stalk (filament) and anther containing pollen.

**STYLE** Connects the ovary to the stigma forming the female reproductive organ.

**SUCCULENT** Juicy moisture-filled foliage.

**SUCKER** A new shoot forms from the root of a parent plant.

**SWALE** A depression between sandhills that becomes a small lake then dries up during drought.

**TOMENTUM** A protective covering on stems or leaves of dense white or grey hair.

**TUBER** Swelling on a root containing food reserves and possibly growth buds.

**ULTRAVIOLET** Light rays beyond the violet end of the spectrum. Visible to insects but invisible to humans.

**VENEER** A thin protective covering — often a waxy coating on a leaf.

**VULNERABLE** At serious risk of vanishing from wild habitats within 20–50 years.

# Acknowledgments

Botanists of the Australian National Botanic Garden, Canberra; Royal Tasmanian Botanic Gardens; Melbourne Herbarium; and Western Australian Herbarium.

Dr Beth Gott, Ethnobotanist, Monash University, Clayton, Victoria.

Leon Costermans, highly respected author and expert on Australian native plants.

Society for Growing Australian Plants.

# Index

110

HOP

## Books

Boden, A. *Floral Emblems of Australia,* Australian National Botanic Gardens, Canberra, 1985

Brooker & Kleinig. *Field Guide To Eucalypts Vol 1,* Inkata, Sydney, 1983

Chippendale, G M. & Johnston R D. *Eucalypts Vol 2,* Nelson, Australia, 1983

Costermans, L. *Native Trees and Shrubs of South-eastern Australia,* Reed New Holland, 2002

Erickson, George, Marchant, & Morcombe. *Flowers and Plants of Western Australia,* Reed, 1973

Greig, D. *Trees of Australia,* New Holland, Sydney, 1998

Greig, D. *Field Guide To Australian Wildflowers,* New Holland, Sydney, 1999

Holliday, I. & Overton, B & D. *Kangaroo Island's Native Plants,* SA, 1994

Holliday, I. *A Field Guide to Melaleucas,* Hamlyn, 1989

Hope, C. *Amazing Facts about Australian Plants,* Steve Parish Publishing, Australia, 2008

Latz, P. *Bushfires and Bushtucker,* A D Press, Alice Springs, 1995

Low, T. *Bush Tucker: Australia's Wild Food Harvest,* Angus & Robertson, 1989

Low, T. *Bush Medicine: A pharmacopoeia of natural remedies,* Collins/Angus & Robertson, 1990

Launceston Field Naturalists Club. (Reprint). *A Guide to Flowers & Plants of Tasmania,* Reed Books Australia, 1992

Petheram, R. & Kok, B. *Plants of the Kimberley Region of Western Australia,* University of Western Australia Press, 1986

Simmon, M. *Acacias of Australia Vol 1,* Nelson, Melbourne, 1987

Symon, D. Jusaitus. M. *Sturt Pea,* Botanic Gardens and State Herbariums, S.A., 2007

Urban, A. *Wildflowers and Plants of Central Australia,* Portside Editions, 1993

Wrigley, J. & Fagg, M. *Australian Native Plants,* Reed New Holland, 1998

## Websites

Australian National Botanic Gardens Canberra
**www.anbg.gov.au**

Australian Flora on Postage Stamps
**www.anbg.gov.au/stamps/index.html**

Society for Growing Australian Plants
**www.asgap.org.au/apol.html**

**www.florabase.calm.wa.gov.au**

**www.austplants.nsw.org.au**

Published by Steve Parish Publishing Pty Ltd
PO Box 1058, Archerfield, Qld 4108 Australia

**www.steveparish.com.au**

ISBN 978174193424 3

First published 2008

Principal Photographer: Steve Parish

Additional photography: M. Fagg/Australian National Botanic Gardens: pp. 33, 59 (top right), 92 & 95 (top); D. Greig/Australian National Botanic Gardens: p. 31; F. Humphreys/Australian National Botanic Gardens: p. 19 (bottom); Stanley Breeden: p. 94; Heather Elson: p. 83; Emma Harm: p. 19 (top left); Greg Harm, SPP; pp. 20 (bottom), 25 (bottom left), 70 & 82; Cathy Hope: pp. 43 (bottom left & bottom centre), 96, 97 (top right), 104 & 107 (centre left & bottom right); Ian Morris: p. 42; Mike & Gayle Quarmby/Outback Pride: p. 95 (bottom)

Front cover: Scarlet Banksia (*Banksia coccinea*)

Title page main image: Red and Green Kangaroo Paws (*Anigozanthos manglesii*)
Inset, top to bottom: Grass-tree (*Xanthorrhoea australis*); Golden Everlasting (*Bracteantha bracteata*)

Text: © Cathy Hope

Editorial: Kerry McDuling; Helen Anderson, Jason Negus & Michele Perry, SPP
Design: Gill Stack, SPP
Image Library: Emma Harm & Clare Thomson, SPP
Production: Tina Brewster, SPP

Prepress by Colour Chiefs Digital Imaging, Brisbane, Australia
Printed in Singapore by Imago

**Produced in Australia at the Steve Parish Publishing Studios**